lovable
LIVABLE
HOME

lovable
LIVABLE
HOME

How to Add Beauty, Get Organized, and Make Your House Work for You

Sherry & John Petersik
of YOUNG HOUSE LOVE

ARTISAN
New York

*To Clara, Teddy, and Burger, who bring
chaos, crumbs, and so much joy to our home.*

Library of Congress Cataloging-in-Publication Data

Petersik, Sherry.
  Lovable livable home : how to add beauty, get organized, and make your house work for you / Sherry and
John Petersik of Young House Love.
     pages cm
Includes bibliographical references and index.
ISBN 978-1-57965-622-5 (alk. paper)
1. Dwellings—Remodeling. 2. Interior decoration. I. Petersik, John. II. Title.
TH4816.P475 2015
645—dc23   2015010991

Design by Toni Tajima

Artisan books are available at special discounts when purchased in bulk for premiums and sales
promotions as well as for fund-raising or educational use. Special editions or book excerpts also can
be created to specification. For details, contact the Special Sales Director at the address below, or send
an e-mail to specialmarkets@workman.com.

Published by Artisan
A division of Workman Publishing Company, Inc.
225 Varick Street
New York, NY 10014-4381
artisanbooks.com

Published simultaneously in Canada by Thomas Allen & Son, Limited

Printed in China
First printing, August 2015

10 9 8 7 6 5 4 3 2 1

CONTENTS

PREFACE

Hey there. We're Sherry and John, and welcome to our book! Actually, welcome to our *second* book. I know. That sounds fancy. But "fancy" is probably the least accurate word to describe us (well, that and maybe "marsupial"). Not sure we've ever felt fancy in our lives. Okay, maybe that time we got cable in our bedroom. That felt pretty crème de la crème.

But in all seriousness, we're pretty much your average couple, raising two kids the best we can while trying to create a beautiful home where we all feel comfortable. The key difference between us and most typical families is that we spent seven years documenting those efforts for the world to see on our blog, *Young House Love.*

It started in 2007 as a do-it-yourself diary to share our first home's kitchen renovation with a few close family members and friends. Despite the fact that we had zero training in DIY, decorating, or even blogging, both our readership and our home projects grew and our little online home diary turned into one big, crazy ride. More than a million people were visiting our site every month. We wrote a best-selling book. We toured the country meeting fans. We designed products sold at places like Target and Home Depot. And we ended up in magazines and newspapers and on TV. Heck, Oprah even mentioned our names at one point (but sadly, they weren't followed by the words "You get a car!").

It was nothing short of insane to two regular Joes like us who simply fell in love with a house and the adventure of making it our own.

And love it we did. For more than four and a half years, we relished turning that fateful first home into a place we adored—a sweet 1,300-square-foot haven that worked awesomely well for the way we lived. It wasn't always easy (there was definitely a fair amount of sweat, tears, and whispered curse words), but that home renovation will go down in history as one of our favorite life adventures. It's what gave us the home renovation bug and led us to tackle two more home makeovers as our family grew. And it's what planted the idea for this book deep in our brains: to show that it's 100 percent possible to create a beautiful and meaningful home that's meant to be lived in and not just looked at.

Yes, after owning three homes with kids and a dog and more crumbs than seems legal (seriously, where do they come from?), we can confidently say that you don't have to sacrifice function for beauty or cover everything in plastic wrap to make it jelly-proof. So if you're ready to let your hair down a little, we're right there with you. There just might be a little paint in ours.

INTRODUCTION

LOVABLE AND LIVABLE is just about the sweetest sweet spot your home can hit. Sure, there might be other adjectives you're hoping to check off too, like colorful, modern, luxe, or bootylicious. But at the end of the day, what's the point of a gorgeous backdrop if you can't settle in and really *live* there? Conversely, giving up on the idea of adding any semblance of beauty or charm and just defaulting purely to utility can lead to all-time-low levels of house satisfaction. Being able to love your surroundings *and* live well within them is the goal, and this book can help you make that happen.

We've filled the following pages with ideas, projects, and makeovers about getting more organized, adding beauty, staying within your budget, and squeezing more function, meaning, and personality out of your home. You'll get to see how we accomplished some of those things in our own house (as well as in a few others), including everything from full-room before and afters, detailed step-by-step tutorials, and quick-and-easy projects you can try in your space.

And since we know there's no one-size-fits-all solution to creating a home, you'll also find tips and pictures from dozens of other families with interesting and inspiring rooms. We have highlighted their home hurdles and how they solved them to make their space work for their family, which, in turn, might work for your home too.

Actually, one of our favorite things about a home's livability and, well, lovability is that everyone's definition is different. Your mailman or your work friends don't have to find your house lovely or livable (in fact, aiming for mass appeal is usually a surefire way to ensure that your home isn't nearly as charming or functional for *you* as it could be). And because tastes and style preferences vary wildly and it's pretty much impossible to find a household that has exactly the same needs and design challenges as yours, we've embraced that by featuring a wide variety of homes and families in these pages.

From big spaces to small ones, from homes with lots of kids, no kids, and furry kids to unique situations like frequent moves with the military, adapting a home for a wheelchair, altering a rental home without fear of losing the security deposit, and downsizing after divorce—it's all here. Seeing these amazing homes and talking to these fascinating families gave us a fresh appreciation for how diverse the definitions of *lovable* and *livable* are. We hope it emboldens you to make your home reflect your family even more and to make it work harder for everyone under your roof.

No book can promise to solve all of your decorating dilemmas or remedy every last one of your family's messes, but we do hope this one helps you check a few big ones off the list, while giving you permission to stop beating yourself up over the rest.

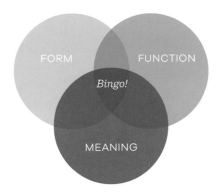

FORM + FUNCTION + MEANING

There's lots of talk of "form and function" in the design world, but we tend to think that focusing only on how something *looks* or how it *works* leaves out a key part of what makes your house *feel* like home. Meaning. That's what's missing. What does something *mean* to you? How does it make you feel?

Maybe it's furniture that has been handed down from your grandparents, or a piece of art drawn by your child. You might even find meaning in a silly kinda-wonky-looking knickknack that you picked up on your honeymoon.

This is an important factor to remember, because putting *meaningful* things into our homes is what makes them uniquely lovable to us. It is what guarantees no home will look or feel the same.

This isn't to say that every item in your home must combine all three attributes to land in the middle of that sweet Venn diagram. Some things in a room may be strictly for looks, others purely for function, while still others solely for the smile they bring to your face. It's definitely extra credit if something checks off two boxes—or even three on occasion—but as long as your rooms are full of items that are beautiful, functional, and meaningful, well, that's pretty much the feel-at-home holy grail.

These three elements are woven throughout the projects and ideas in the book, from hardworking solutions to pretty design ideas and personal touches that can help you put your family's stamp on a home.

WHAT'S IN THIS BOOK

Lovable Livable Home is broken into seven chapters representing the spaces most typically found in a home—everything from big common areas (kitchens and living rooms) to small and private ones (like foyers, bathrooms, and bedrooms). Not every idea will apply to your situation or style preferences, especially since we included some pretty one-of-a-kind rooms, so don't hesitate to skip, jump around, or flip through the book to zero in on whatever grabs you.

FRESH UPDATES AT OUR HOUSE

We've recently tackled a few major room overhauls (no more blue trim in the dining room!), as well as some weekend makeovers, smaller sentimental projects, and organizational updates. We couldn't be more excited to share before and afters of how we've transformed our home—including our once dark living room—into a place that feels just like us *and* works wonderfully for our family of five (Chihuahua included).

PROJECTS AND HOW-TOS

We're do-it-yourselfers at heart, so there are projects peppered throughout this book, many complete with step-by-step instructions. We know DIY can be intimidating, so we've included some easy updates (those sport a Quickie Project label at the top), along with more detailed tutorials that might take an afternoon or a weekend to complete. From a simple way to hang coffee mugs in the kitchen to a desk organizer made from bungee cords, these projects are a great way to dip your toe into the made-it-myself waters and make small changes that will have a big impact on your home.

BIG DESIGN IDEAS

Sometimes solving our at-home challenges calls for major updates, so we've also packed the chapters with larger-scale design tricks, renovation ideas, and decorating tips, including examples of how we and other homeowners put them into practice. Many of these are things you can tackle on your own, but some may call for the help of a professional or two, depending on your skill set and comfort level. There's no shame in asking for help when you need it, so don't let the idea of hiring a professional hold you back.

HOMEOWNER PROFILES

One of the most fascinating parts of this process for us was talking to families from around the country (and the world!) and hearing what they struggle with and how they handle their home challenges. We've included photos and tips from dozens of homes and highlighted a bunch of families as a reminder that we all have different challenges and there are a variety of solutions out there waiting to be discovered.

SURVEY STATS

Since there's no way to truly represent every type of home and family within our book's pages, we cast an even wider net by conducting an online poll. More than 35,000 people (!!!) weighed in, and you'll get to see some of the results of this survey running across the bottom of some pages (like this one). It's a fun way for you to see what situations, challenges, and preferences you might have in common with the masses—or what sets you and your home apart.

survey says: The homes of the 35,000 people we polled ranged from 250 square feet to over 10,000, with the average home being around 1,800 square feet.

LIVING SPACES

John says

WE'VE NEVER REALLY BEEN "two living rooms" kind of people. In fact, the formal living room in our first house basically became a glorified hallway with a couch and a fireplace in it—as in, most of the time we spent in there was when we were passing through.

Of course, that may change once our kids get older and we have a greater need for a space for the tweens to chillax (or whatever they're calling it by then) while we grown-ups stay out of their hair, but for now, we're much happier to convert a secondary "formal living room" into something we'll use a lot more, like a larger dining room (in the case of our second house) or a home office (like we have in our current house).

Hanging personal photos and art around our TV takes the focus off that big black box.

Besides generally being fans of using all of the rooms in our house (and changing their function if the ones we inherit don't make sense for our family), we also like having one big family-friendly living space where everyone can hang out comfortably. Sure, it may mean a bit more chaos and mess than if we had a kid-free lounging space just for adults or evening entertaining, and we may not all enjoy the same TV shows all the time (this means you and your *Real Housewives,* Sherry), but for the most part we actually *like* sharing our living space with one another and carving out a few everyone-friendly updates to make the room work well for all of us.

For example, our dark sectional boasts enough space for everyone to sprawl out and stands up to our dog Burger's little claws, and its slipcover can be removed and washed whenever it needs to be (blueberries and baby spit are no match for this guy). It's not the fanciest sofa by any stretch, but it's just right for us at this stage of our lives.

We also have a big white ottoman in place of a traditional coffee table. It's soft enough that we don't worry about kids face-planting into it, and the leather upholstery wipes clean without a second thought. Plus, it opens to reveal tons of hidden toy storage, so it's pretty much a triple threat.

Speaking of toys, we've always been down with using our living room as a play zone too. Whether it's with a basket of toys in a corner (or even the dollhouse and the art table that we kept in our last living room), making these spaces play-friendly has been a great way to keep the family together—even if it means occasionally stepping on a Lego or sitting on a squeaky toy.

In this chapter you'll also see how a smattering of other families are living in these broadly defined "living spaces," including many others who want their kids and pets to peacefully coexist without making too many major style concessions.

An oversized basket next to the armchair makes for pretty easy toy cleanup.

Our **Living Room** Makeover

We love the coziness of a dark living room, but without as much natural light as the rest of the rooms in our house (thanks to windows that overlook a shaded back porch), ours often felt more gloomy than relaxing. With a little sweat equity and a lot of paint, we slowly transformed it into the bright and welcoming living space we'd always pictured. Turn the page to see how we did it!

Before

☀ SPRAYED THE TRIM.
We're suckers for white wainscoting and beams, so after protecting the rest of the room with cardboard and taped-off drop cloths, we used a paint sprayer and a couple of gallons of stain-blocking primer and semigloss paint (Simply White by Benjamin Moore) to create some easy-to-wipe-down surfaces that bounce a lot more light around while playing off the rich wood floors.

☀ WENT WHITE ON THE WALLS. After initially painting the walls warm gray and doing a light whitewashing on the brick, we decided there were too many surfaces with too many different colors and textures going on for our liking (a wall of brick + a ceiling full of beams + three half-planked walls = a lot of lines going in every direction). So we unified things with the same white paint, which helps all of the textures work together.

☀ FURNISHED AND ACCESSORIZED. With the exception of a colorful new rug and a few small touches, like bamboo blinds and a branch mirror, everything in the room was something we already had. All the pieces look more inviting in our brighter and happier living space, and we love how the white walls are warmed up by the wood furniture and colorful accents.

Fired things up.
The original mantel felt unsubstantial and chopped the room in half, which dwarfed the space (it needed height, not width!). So we built a new, chunkier one that feels a little grander (it was inspired by one that we constructed in our previous home). We splurged on a gas insert but offset some of the cost by hunting down remnant marble pieces for the surround and installing them ourselves.

(continued)

✳ GOT BLUE. The white beams overhead quickly stole our hearts, so we went one step further and accented them by painting the ceiling a fresh greeny-blue color (Galt Blue by Benjamin Moore). It brings some personality into the room and makes our standard 8-foot ceilings feel higher too.

✳ GILDED THE BUILT-IN. Painted backs are one of our favorite tricks for de-blanding a bookcase, and they can be completed in just a few hours with a quart of paint. This time, instead of using wall paint, we added some subtle metallic sheen with all-purpose acrylic craft paint that's meant to work on walls, furniture, or accent pieces (DecoArt Elegant Finish in Champagne Gold). We applied it with a paintbrush, working in long vertical strokes from the top of the bookcase to the bottom, since short choppy strokes can show. It took four coats, so don't let the first one scare you (it'll start out really spotty!), but now we've got some warm understated sparkle that was so cheap to add (just five dollars for that pot of paint). Plus, if you don't like the result, it's easier to undo than metallic wallpaper!

The shelves look nice and all, but where's the ceramic Chihuahua?

The Mix: Color + Pattern + Texture

Look at any room you love (whether it's in your home or in a magazine) and you'll likely see three key design elements at play—color, pattern, and texture. It takes some practice to find the mix that you like best (it's different for everyone), but it's a helpful trio to keep in mind if a space feels off or incomplete. Does your room have too much of one category (like competing colors, for example)? Is it entirely lacking in another (like no texture anywhere, which can make the room feel flat)? It takes some experimenting to achieve the proper balance, so a little trial and error might help you hit the right notes.

Color. If you're nervous about going overboard in the color department, let one item be the star. In their sunroom (opposite), Christi and Barrett layered an over-dyed Persian rug on top of the carpet to inject some color and define the seating area. Try adding color through rugs, pillows, small furniture, or accessories.

Pattern. This room is a perfect example of one focal piece (the rug) boasting both a bold color and pattern, which layers in nicely with the more subtle textures and materials in the rest of the space. Other items like pillows, art, or even an accent wall can combine color and pattern too.

Texture. This room has a layered mix of textures going on, from the soft billowy curtains and painted brick wall to the woven sea-grass carpeting and tufted leather ottoman. You can add texture with curtains, large furniture, bamboo blinds, rugs, and lighting.

Put a **Pin** in It

In our house, we have a map of the United States that's mounted onto cork backing and poked full of pins to mark the places our family has traveled. And once we've traveled more of the world, we'll upgrade to a globe like the one below. The spinning sphere is cardboard, so it's easy to push pins into, and the flags we added to large pins make it easier to see all of the lands we have (hypothetically) ventured to.

We made these flags by wrapping washi tape around map pins from a home-office supply shop. Once the tape was secured around each pin, we cut the long rectangular flaps into triangles.

Making Hand-Me-Down Furniture Work

We get that "what do I do with hand-me-downs I might not love as-is" question all the time. And it's pretty dicey to answer because so much depends on the piece (what it is, how ill-fitting it is, how valuable an antique it might be, and what meaning it holds) and the person you inherited it from (what their expectations are, how they might react to your use, and so on). Here are some ideas for handling that hand-me-down.

✳ **Try embracing the mix.** Most rooms actually benefit from having pieces of a slightly different style or time period layered in, so mixing things up may do your space more good than you expect. You can help integrate an older piece into a room by putting some more-modern items on it (and vice versa: Put some older accessories on your newer furniture). Switching out hardware to tie in to something else in the room can help too.

✳ **Refinish it.** In many cases, the person who passed down the item to you won't mind if you adapt it to make it work for your space. You might try updating the piece with paint, fresh stain, or any other treatment that you think would help it live more happily in your home.

✳ **Focus on the meaning.** Some pieces can't add to a room design-wise, no matter how hard you try to make them. But if they bring personal meaning to you, they add something that you can't buy at the store. This may be the item —even if it's out of scale or gaudily finished—that becomes a conversation piece or reminds you of the beloved person who passed it along to you.

✳ **Pass it on.** If you truly have no room, use, or appreciation for it, the person who handed down the item might prefer to see it get used and loved again, rather than end up in storage or cast off somewhere. If that's the case, it may be better off in the hands of another relative or friend. Try to emphasize this to the gifter, and be willing to participate in finding it another home.

✳ **Hack it.** No, we don't mean hack it to bits, but there may be just one part of the hand-me-down that you can work with and love. For example, if a buffet has an attached hutch that's not useful in your space, you could remove it and add a new stone top to the buffet. You could even rescue pretty hardware from a broken dresser, or snag the little gold caster wheels off an uncomfortable desk chair. Check out our hand-me-down remake on the next page for another idea.

Make a **Drawer Shelf**

This wall shelf was once a hand-me-down nightstand that was too beat up to use (our relatives were planning to scrap it), but we swooped in to save part of it.

1 Remove the drawer and any hardware (knobs, drawer slides, etc.).

2 Determine the new depth you'd like for your shelf (ours is 4 inches deep); mark both sides of the drawer.

3 We used a **table saw**, but you can also carefully cut along those lines—through both sides and the base panel—with a handsaw. Use clamps to hold the drawer in place while you cut.

4 Pry or cut off the back panel of the drawer as cleanly as possible. If it doesn't come off cleanly, you may need to purchase a new piece of wood to create the back. (Ours, thankfully, came off easily.)

5 Sand the cut edges of your drawer to remove any rough spots with **medium-grit sandpaper.**

6 Apply a thin bead of **wood glue** along the cut back edge of your drawer. Place the end panel back onto the drawer and carefully nail it in place with small finishing nails. Allow the glue to dry.

7 If this doesn't feel secure, consider adding **L-brackets** or small corner braces to the back and underside of the drawer to strengthen the attachment.

8 Nail two **sawtooth hangers** to the back of the drawer (one on each side).

9 Hang the drawer using **screws** driven directly into a stud or anchors.

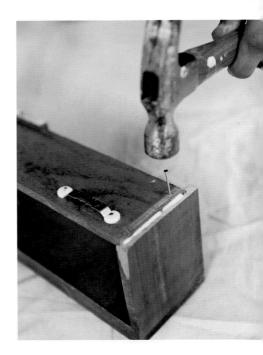

Pick an
Inspiration Piece

If you're feeling stuck about where to start with your room, one great way to break the ice and get moving is to find a piece that you love, even if it's not within your budget or even for sale anymore. It may be a rug or a painting that can instantly help you choose a color palette for the room, or it might be a must-have armoire that guides the style and finish of your other furnishings. For Abby and Tait, it was a woven patio chair that wasn't literally going to live in their house, but which inspired the entire vibe they wanted in their vacation home. Once it was selected as their inspiration, the combination of casual white fabrics paired with woven and natural elements was easy to pull together—and it all came from that little old chair.

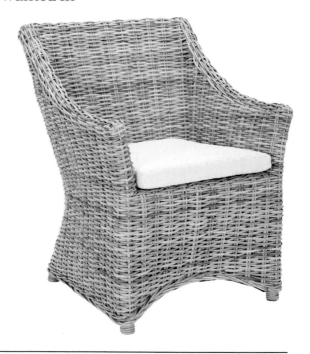

Bring In Something **Bright**

You can be bold without putting a saturated color on your wall. So whether you just love the neutral paint that's already in your room or you're a renter who can't change it, here are three other places to add a big ol' serving of hue.

1 RUGS. Elisabeth added hot-pink rugs to inject a whole lot of happy into her living room. She couldn't find a big square rug that she loved for the space, so she paired two rectangular ones to create the perfect fit. The decorative edges and centrally placed coffee table help them feel unified and intentional instead of randomly cobbled together.

Find the right sized rug.
A too-small rug can make a room feel unbalanced and cramped, so try to choose something that helps to define the entire living zone and allows at least all of the front legs of the seating arrangement to rest on it, rather than look like they're loitering around something they're not allowed to touch.

(continued)

1

2

2 FURNITURE. Aletha and Greg chose a cobalt sectional to add serious vibrancy to their home's stacked brick accent wall, but if you're not ready to commit to color on such a large piece, consider an interestingly patterned armchair or even a colorful ottoman or pouf. They're less expensive, and there are tons of fun options out there.

3 WINDOWS. Window treatments can take a room from "getting there" to "hey now, that's polished"—whether you're adding dramatic floor-length curtains or a simple roman shade. Because Sunny and Read's sectional precluded long curtains, they installed two large valances that add color and a playful-yet-tailored element to the room.

Seven Ways to Make Your Living Room **Kid-Friendly**

Like us, most of the families we visited didn't have separate formal and casual living rooms. But that didn't mean every living space we saw was overrun with toys and kid stuff. In fact, we came across a bunch of seemingly elegant and adult-looking rooms that we were surprised to learn were the only living area and, yes, kids spent lots of time in them.

Note: We use the term *kid-friendly* to indicate durability, cleanability, or general survivability in the war our kids seemingly wage on our things. But that "friendly" part of the term is important, since it reminds us that our spaces shouldn't just be kid-proof, but also can be inviting and comfortable for our kids as well.

1 **INVEST IN STYLISH STORAGE.** These graphic ottomans in Jenny's living room bring a classic pattern to her home's only living space, while giving her kids a place to stash stuff.

2 **GIVE 'EM THE SLIP.** Spare yourself expensive upholstery cleaning by considering pieces with slipcovers, which can get tossed into the wash. You'll find great options—even modern, tailored-looking ones—at nearly every retailer. Plus, you can replace them down the line with a new color or pattern without paying for a whole new chair or sofa. If you freak out at the thought of kids on a white sofa, relax. Time and time again we hear parents praise the simplicity of removing stains from white fabrics (using everything from OxiClean or bleach to stain-removal pens and even simply air-drying in the sun).

(continued)

3 MIX HIGH AND LOW, LITERALLY. Combining high-end pieces with more affordable ones is a great trick for making a room look more expensive. Monica and Dean do it by keeping the high-end things—like this antique chandelier—above the action and out of reach. Meanwhile, items like the secondhand sofa and acrylic coffee table can survive just fine below.

4 LOOK AT LEATHER. Not only can leather lend rooms everything from a tailored modern vibe to a rustic vintage look, it also wipes down wonderfully, and wear just adds to its patina.

5 ACRYLIC TAKES A BEATING TOO. It gives a room the sophistication of glass, without that pesky I-will-shatter-everywhere part of the equation. Plus, it wipes clean and helps a room feel less cluttered.

(continued)

Joey and Jeff wanted to visually separate the living room and kitchen, so they built in a daybed that's planked with reclaimed wood. Not only has it become a favorite reading spot for their girls, but there's also a hidden playhouse above it!

4

5

6 BE SMART ABOUT SURFACES. With young kids in the mix, the coffee table may not be the best spot for a breakable heirloom. Lisa and Mike keep accessible surfaces kid-friendly and staggered floating shelves from Ikea for a custom-looking display that adds some polish while still being play-friendly.

7 USE BUILT-INS TO YOUR ADVANTAGE. Pieces that mix open and closed storage are great for kid-friendly living rooms. You can rely on the concealed areas for toys and games and use the open shelves to showcase favorite accessories.

AND REMEMBER, BE REALISTIC. If you're living with young kids, it may not be the best time to go out and buy the most expensive couch or the most breakable lamps of your lifetime. But that doesn't mean your favorite decor (yes, even some of that expensive and breakable stuff) has to stay packed away until your nest is empty and you should just accept that your home will look like a day-care facility until then. It's all about knowing your family and figuring out where you can successfully integrate pieces that lend sophistication with those that can stand up to heavy use.

survey says: 80% of the people we polled don't have both a "formal" and a "casual" living room— and of the 20% that do have a formal one, most said they spend time there "very infrequently."

Keepin' It **Pet-Friendly**

Like children, our furry four-legged friends are important family members to consider when creating a home, especially one that doesn't leave you stressed out all the time. Our Chihuahua, Burger, packs a pretty light punch (he doesn't do much gnawing and doesn't have much hair to shed), but we've still made quite a few choices with him in mind (and we accept that all our throw pillows will eventually have a nap dent).

Here are some tips we learned from pet owners who have bigger (and furrier) challenges to manage.

1 TEST WOOD SURFACES. Anna and Liam know their love of midcentury modern furniture isn't always a

great mix with their two cats' claws, so they test every piece to make sure the wood isn't too soft. (If a fingernail can make a dent, it's not durable enough.) It's not a perfect system, but they've learned to strategically place blankets to hide existing damage and to discourage more.

2 TAKE FABRICS FOR A TEST DRIVE. Carrie and Matt's dogs, Marco and Atticus (seen in

the paintings above the couch), are welcome on any furniture, so when the couple went shopping for their first "grown-up" couch, they made sure to bring upholstery samples home to test against their furry-children's claws. The winner was this tightly woven microfiber sectional from West Elm, which is holding up great to the dogs, and even Sprocket the cat.

(continued)

Hide the litter box.

To help get the litter box (and its smell) out of the house, Hillary and Scott bought and fixed up an old cabinet from the Habitat for Humanity ReStore to house the litter in the garage. The cats access it through a hole in the back that connects to a pet door installed inside the house, which keeps everyone—including the kitties—much happier.

3 BEWARE OF FLOOR WEAR. Emily and Todd rescued Tucker after they'd already chosen light-colored bamboo floors for their home. Even a hard wood like bamboo can scratch under his eighty-five-pound body, but they're grateful that the light stain makes the damage less visible than a dark stain would have.

4 GIVE THEM THEIR OWN SPACE. Anna and Liam's cats love curling up in baskets, so Anna tries to keep a bunch in the house so the cats have their own spaces to spend time in—and therefore spend less time on the furniture.

5 INVEST IN A VACUUM CLEANER THAT YOUR WHOLE FAMILY CAN USE. While strong suction is important, the vacuum should be very easy to operate and access. A cheapo vacuum cleaner that gets used often beats a high-tech vacuum cleaner that only an adult can operate.

6 STAY ON TOP OF VACUUMING. Liam has committed himself to being a diligent vacuumer (up to three times per week) because it prevents pet hair from building up on or matting into the furniture, which becomes more challenging to tackle the longer it sits.

7 KEEP A HANDHELD VAC IN A CONVENIENT LOCATION. Handheld vacuums are great for quick cleanups and for kids who need an easy chore, so Hillary keeps one in the kitchen pantry.

8 SET A CLEANUP SCHEDULE. Hillary and Scott's kids clean out their guinea pig and mouse enclosures every Saturday morning and have set days for litter box duties too. Their philosophy is "Don't wait until you can smell the animals before you clean up after them!"

(continued)

Who run the world? Dogs.

survey says: 75% of the pet owners we polled say they allow their pets on the couch.

9 STASH CLEANING SUPPLIES AROUND THE HOUSE. You'll be more likely to take care of a pet accident if you don't have to go upstairs to fetch a rag and spray, so Hillary keeps some stocked under every sink.

10 ACCEPT IT. Generally the pet owners we talked to try not to worry themselves silly about wear and tear, since it's an inevitable part of having a furry family member. As with having children, know where you may need to make compromises for your pets and then do your best to stop stressing and enjoy them.

Pets a Plenty

Hillary and Scott
live with
Brynn (age 11), Callie (age 9), Libbie and Lola (the dogs), Anna and Lyle (the cats), Olga and Stella (the guinea pigs), and Luna (the mouse)
and describe their home as
Functional, Casual, and Quiet

In addition to their two daughters, Hillary and Scott have seven pets. *Seven.* Two dogs, two cats, two guinea pigs, and a mouse. Oh, did we mention they recently fostered five puppies on top of that? But living with so many creatures has taught this family a few tricks about keeping their pets *and* their sanity. Side note: Can you believe they describe their house as quiet?!

Adapt floors for easy cleaning.
Hillary and Scott's daughter Callie has two guinea pigs and the mess of pine shavings on the floor to prove it. So they recently tore out the old carpet and then patched, primed, painted, and sealed the subfloor to make sweeping up easier. It's a temporary measure until they can install hardwood floors, but it has already made a world of difference. Hillary also built a rolling platform to easily get the cage out of the way when it's time to clean up.

survey says: 48% of the pet owners we polled let their furry friends sleep in bed with them.

Where Oh Where to **Put the TV**

If you're anything like us, a television is a must-have in a living space. And with increasingly slim profiles, sleek designs, and wire-free solutions, the ol' boob tube has never been easier to integrate. TVs and TV placement are surprisingly polarizing topics (some people loathe a TV over a fireplace with a passion), so just weigh the pros and cons of each option, and go with whatever feels best for your family.

1 SITTING ON FURNITURE

Pro: Easy to set up, and many media stands create a natural spot to hide cable boxes and wires.

Con: Can eat up precious floor space and create tipping hazards if not properly secured.

2 HIDDEN IN AN ARMOIRE OR A CABINET

Pro: Blends into a room where you don't want to call attention to it.

Con: The size of the furniture limits the size of the TV, and you have to open and close the doors for use.

3 MOUNTED ON THE WALL

Pro: Frees up floor space and can nest nicely into a frame collage to help it blend in.

Con: Mounting can be tricky, plus it requires ingenuity for hiding the wires and boxes.

4 MOUNTED ABOVE A FIREPLACE

Pro: Combining a room's focal points can make furniture arrangements easier.

Con: May require the TV to be hung higher than is comfortable for viewing.

survey says: Where do people keep their TVs? After "sitting on furniture" (41%) came "mounted on the wall" (17%), while "above a fireplace" earned 8% and "hidden in an armoire or a cabinet" got 4%.

Expand Your **Media Cabinet** Horizons

Don't limit yourself to searching "media cabinet" when hunting for something to plop your TV on. You can get the same function out of a variety of more interesting pieces, like dressers, buffets, and consoles—like this cool card catalog base that Cate and Frank use in their living room (opposite). Here's what you should look for when shopping for your own makeshift media cabinet.

✳ A sturdy piece of furniture that's not too tall (between 22 and 34 inches is a good rule of thumb—or just aim to place the middle of the TV at your eye level when you're sitting on the couch).

✳ The piece should be at least 20 percent wider than your TV, otherwise your screen may dwarf its base.

✳ It's a nice bonus to find a piece with open shelves or glass-front cabinet doors for your cable box and other components.

Can't find a spot for the cable box? Get an IR receiver. Our living room TV sits on a dresser, and we didn't like keeping the components on top or shoved on the floor under it. So we ordered a sixteen-dollar infrared receiver online. It plugs into the back of most cable boxes and the cord extends to wherever you want to point your remote (like the front of your TV), which frees you up to hide components behind a solid door or in a drawer. Just remember to drill vent holes in the back so the components don't overheat.

survey says: 44% of the people we polled have a TV in their bedroom.

Take Focus off the **TV**

We love staring at the television as much as the next DIYer, but when it's turned off, you'll want something to distract from its sheer black-hole-iness. We have a collage of picture frames surrounding ours, and here are a couple of other ideas to try.

Built-In Shelves

By nestling their TV in wall-to-wall bookcases, Joey and Jeff made it one element of many instead of the main event, which is perfect for this family that only occasionally turns on the TV.

Accent Wall

Lisa and Mike hung store-bought pine boards on the wall behind their basement TV to create this planked feature. It makes it easy to hide wires, plus the built-in storage cabinets and ventless gas fireplace add plenty of eye candy below.

How to Talk Someone Into a Purchase

When I find an item for our house that I love, I tend to fall for it hard. But John can be slower to come around. So I occasionally find myself in the position of making a case for why something should come home with us. If that sounds familiar, here are four tips and tactics I am happy to share.

1 Do your research.
You don't want to seem impulsive, so find other similar items and show why they're not a perfect fit. (Maybe they're more expensive or not the right size.) This will demonstrate what a special find your new object is and why you might want to pounce on it right away. I especially love doing this with thrift-store or Craigslist finds, since they're easy to compare to similar store versions that are sold at full price.

2 Paint a picture. Detail exactly what you'll use the item for, where you'll put it, and what it will add to your lives. (For example:

"We can put this bench next to our door to store shoes and boots, so they're not strewn all over the floor.") This will show it's a rational purchase, not just an emotional one.

3 Make cents of things.
Since John and I don't like spending frivolously or buying things we can't afford, when I really think something would be a great addition to our home, I'm prepared to make a financial case for it. Knowing how the purchase fits into our budget and being ready to whip out examples of where we've saved in other areas (or what else I'm willing to

sacrifice for the item) can help to accommodate a new purchase.

4 Get your hands dirty.
Sometimes John is hesitant to agree to something because he fears he'll be the one stuck assembling, hanging, or hauling it on his own. By being willing to chip in and do it with him, or even volunteering to do the work myself (which might mean taking on assembly, recruiting a friend/relative to haul it with me, and even offering to undo something if it doesn't work out—like a new paint job) always helps.

Do these tactics work all the time? No. Heck, sometimes I even talk myself out of a purchase after going through these steps. But they do go a long way toward having a productive conversation about the items *we* bring into *our* home, and they can make a giant difference in John's excitement level about something. Because ultimately we both want to invest in things thoughtfully, so our house is full of things we both love.

How to Talk Someone Out of a Purchase

Occasionally I find myself in the precarious position of telling Sherry why I think something she wants to buy should probably stay at the store. In an effort to not always be the bad guy, I've got four tricks for making her think twice about that "must-have pillow" that might not really be better than all of the other "must-have pillows" we already own.

1 Ask specific questions. "Where are we going to put it?" "What are we going to do with what's already there?" "Do you think this is the best price?" If quick and clear answers don't arise, it might help expose an impulse purchase—or at least encourage someone to think it through a bit more.

2 Have an opinion. Your opinion won't carry much weight if you're always giving a halfhearted, "No, I don't like it." Try offering specific feedback—"I feel like it's kind of big," or "Do you think red is the best color?" Show that your resistance is grounded in something real, not just a general opposition to change or spending money.

3 Know your stuff. The oft-used "Don't we already have one like that?" defense may have a low success rate if it's a bluff, but if you can cite a specific item ("We've already got that big serving platter we used last Thanksgiving, don't we?"), it'll be harder to sneak something by you.

4 Distract. No, don't throw a smoke bomb (well, actually that might work . . .). Instead, draw attention to something bigger you've been pining for. A new rug? A kitchen reno? A vacation? Setting your sights on a larger purchase can make an impulse buy seem less important by comparison and redirect you both to the bigger goal at hand.

While these tricks have saved us a fair amount of money over the years, it's also good to remember that not every purchase needs to be a super-rational one. Sometimes giving in to an item just because you know it'll make your other half happy is all the reason you need. And you know what? It feels great to be the good guy every now and then.

I'm always in support of treat purchases.

Show Off Your Relationship with Books

We're not talking about some PDA between you and your favorite tome (unless that's your thing, I guess). We all have different relationships with books—some people are occasional readers who mostly borrow from the library, while others are voracious bookworms who take pride in displaying their growing collection. The great news is, wherever you fall, books are one of the coolest things to incorporate into your home. Here are some of our favorite tips for displaying them.

* **MIX IN OTHER OBJECTS.** Unless you have enough to fill an entire bookcase for that old library feel, you can break up your shelves with things like vases, decorative boxes, or even potted plants to keep things looking full but not too cluttered.

* **THINK HORIZONTAL.** You can also add variety by laying small stacks of books on their backs to break things up.

* **GO NAKED.** Many times if you remove the dust jackets you'll reveal colorful woven spines, which can add interest to any room.

* **ADD A COLORFUL BACKDROP.** Paint the backs of your bookcases for an easy way to make the books and objects on them pop. It's especially great on built-ins, but can be used on freestanding cases too.

* **DON'T BE TOO FUSSY.** Books are awesome, especially en masse. So don't go overboard trying to make perfect stacks or completely balanced displays. Some of the coolest bookcases we've seen are chock-full of good reads without too much rhyme or reason to the display. It's a really authentic and inviting look, so don't try too hard.

Make **Statement Storage**

Like books, many other objects that you own can be stored in interesting ways that add beauty and function to your rooms (two birds, meet stone). Heck, you may even get to show off a meaningful collection in the process. So . . . three birds?

Think orderly.
Hanging items in grids can help things look more artful and organized, like these extra bike tires that Emily and Todd hung in their basement. It solved a storage dilemma (they are garage-less), and it makes converting their mountain bikes to their road-ready state a lot more convenient since they can easily see everything and grab the right tire faster.

Accent with paint.
This nook turned out to be the perfect spot for Joey and Jeff to hang their instruments. Painting the back wall blue not only complements the wood tones but highlights the grouping even more.

Use Paint to **Highlight Architecture**

If you're at a loss for what to accent in a room, try looking at its inherent features. A nice high ceiling or traditional wainscoting might benefit from some paint to make sure no one overlooks your home's inherent awesomeness.

Go colorful.
Sarah and Peter wanted more cheer in the living room of their small home in Sweden. Adding pink paint to their fireplace was a spur-of-the-moment solution that has done just the trick.

Go dark.
Accents don't always have to be colorful. Deep wood stains or even dark paint can make a feature pop. Emily and Shane painted all of their interior doors black to bring some elegant contrast to their mostly white home.

Five Ways to Add Aged Elegance

If you've got a room that's feeling too "new"—like you just took everything in it out of the box—try bringing in some aged textures or vintage pieces to give it more of a collected-over-time vibe. Here are five ideas to consider.

1 CLASSIC ARMCHAIRS. With details like curved arms or full skirts, these can turn up the elegance factor, and can be found on Craigslist or at yard sales.

2 AN ANTIQUE LIGHT. Or even a new one that looks aged is a fun and unexpected addition to a sitting area. This one is hardwired and hangs from a wall-mounted hook, but a wire-free lantern with a candle inside is sweet too, and extra simple to hang.

3 RAW PLANKS. From chunky overhead beams to a full ceiling's worth of wood, these can add interest and warmth to any formerly boxy or characterless space.

4 A CONCRETE PLANTER. An old one with a family crest or vintage markings on it brings aged charm and some life to a room, thanks to the indoor plant it houses.

5 A GORGEOUS OLD RUG. They can add tons of texture and pattern to a room, and can be found on places like eBay and even Craigslist without breaking the bank.

A ceramic animal is always a welcome addition in our book. (Literally, since this is our book.)

Open-Space Living

Wendy
lives with
Owen (the dog)
and describes her studio loft as
Eclectic, Whimsical, and Evolving

Once her kids, Tess and Max, grew up and left the nest, Wendy took the leap to downsize from her single-family home to an urban one-room loft that is less than a third of the size. Her biggest challenge was creating a few defined spaces within a studio, something she'd never faced in her house. Here are some of her tricks.

1 LOOK FOR ANY ARCHITECTURE THAT CAN BE YOUR GUIDE. With no walls to create zones and inform furniture placement, Wendy turned to the space's three large windows and wood ceiling beams to anchor three different areas: a sleeping zone, a living area, and a work space.

2 CREATE VISUAL DIVISION. To give her sleeping space a sense of separation from the living area nearby, she strategically used furniture—like a screen made from old doors and a four-poster bed—to define the bedroom.

3 USE TABLES AND RUGS AS CENTERPIECES. Wendy anchored both her living and her work area with a table and a rug. They're both large rectangular items that made it easy to place other furniture around them.

I'll have what he's having.

Thanks for the **Memories** . . . Now Where Do I Put Them?

We're sentimental creatures, and having adorable children who grow up too darn fast has us on the brink of becoming memento hoarders. So if you're on the path to a keepsake intervention, here are two ideas to consider.

1 **A BOX-Y SOLUTION.** When our old storage method (a shoe box) started overflowing, we upgraded to three larger simple plastic bins. We use one for our keepsakes (love letters, race medals, an old dog toy that Burger ripped the face off of—you know, the usual). The other two house items for each kid, like birth announcements and hospital bracelets. Our daughter, Clara, even helped us draw the labels, which we attached with bright tape. They're like keepsakes adorning our keepsakes. Oh geez, here come the waterworks.

2 A CATALOG TURNED TIME CAPSULE. Sara and Jason scored this card catalog at a local college library sale and now it serves as a giant time capsule in their living room. They fill one drawer per year with items that don't fit in their photo albums (pressed leaves, shells, ticket stubs, etc.) and review them on New Year's Eve as an annual family tradition.

Cute **Clay House Ornaments**

A few years ago we hung up our trendy themed-Christmas-tree hats and decided to stick with a mishmash of personal ornaments. Now every year we try to add—and make!—new things for our sweet smorgasbord of a tree. The homes we've lived in are a big part of our family's story, so we decided to honor each one in clay. Here's how you can do it too.

1 Roll **clay** (we used white Sculpey Oven-Bake Clay) into flat slabs and place the pieces on a protected flat surface (like **cardboard covered with wax paper**).

2 Use a **craft knife** to cut the basic shapes of the house, like a big rectangle for the walls, a trapezoid for the roof, and a smaller rectangle for the door.

3 Join together the basic house elements, and then add other distinguishing features like a chimney or porch columns (we used a small square-shaped **drill bit** to make little imprints for windows and a wire to add crosshatched details to the brick facade).

4 Be sure to poke a hole in the top to accommodate a **ribbon** (for hanging).

5 Bake it in the oven according to the clay's instructions.

6 When the house is cured, you can paint it. We went with pearly white to add some holiday shimmer, and then accented each ornament with that home's front door color.

Get a **Living Room Vibe** Outside

Jamie and AJ's condo was short on space for their large family, so extending their livable area to the covered deck outside was a must. Here's how they gave a decidedly outdoor space more of an interior feel.

✳ ADDED CURTAINS.
Jamie hung five-dollar drop cloths on PVC piping that she spray painted gold to cozy things up. Now the room is useful even when it's rainy—they just slide the curtains shut.

✳ DRESSED UP THE WALL.
Jamie used washi tape heated with a blow dryer to make outdoor siding look more like wallpaper (the heat helps it stick long-term).

✳ PAINTED THE FLOOR.
Jamie and AJ used porch paint to add a striped pattern that mimics one big area rug.

Living Large in a Condo

Jamie and AJ
live with
Sophia (age 11), Etienne (age 9), Charlotte (age 6), Laurent (age 3), Nicasio (age 3), and Oliver and Audrey (the dogs)
and describe their home as
Functional, Eclectic, and Energetic

Jamie and AJ live in what they call "semi-controlled chaos" with their two dogs and five children, three of whom were adopted from Ethiopia. But they've managed to put their own stamp on a builder-grade condo while maximizing their condo's square footage.

EATING SPACES

Sherry says

SOMETIMES WE EAT LUNCH in our office, so I should probably clarify that traditional eating spaces—i.e., kitchens and dining rooms—are what this chapter is about, not all of the spaces in your house where you eat (because if you're us, that means just about everywhere but the bathrooms . . . we do have *some* standards).

Kitchens can be simultaneously awesome and maddening. Full of storage, yet hopelessly disorganized. Equally exciting and daunting to renovate. For some families a kitchen is a room full of stuff (gadgets, spatulas, and pans galore), and for others it might be a place where little to no meal prep actually happens—except for a phone call to the pizza guy.

One kitchen update we've already tackled? Organizing our pantry to place kid snacks within kid reach.

We're still building up steam (and savings) to tackle a full-blown kitchen reno in our current house. It's not that we aren't dying to get rid of the faux-brick vinyl floor and the 5-inch-deep kitchen sink (think about that depth for a second; even a water glass sticks up above the lip)—it's just that with a space that's so central to our home and our daily lives, well, we want to get it right. And in our case that means living with our current kitchen for a nice long time before rushing into a reno that isn't as well planned as it could be. (We still can't decide what type of counter we want!)

That's why we're fans of "Phase One." We think of Phase One as a low-key, low-cost, and low-commitment update to a room, which gives you permission to experiment and try solutions on for size before diving into a more costly renovation. It takes some extra patience and a little extra dough to do a Phase One update instead of leaping into your final redo, but we've found that not only is it a helpful step in identifying what you want most from your spaces, it can also show you what you don't want (which can save you some major money, time, and heart-wrenching regret in the end).

Our current kitchen is a great example of this, and we know our Phase One updates have saved us from some costly mistakes that would be difficult to undo if we tried them during a full renovation. For one, we have always admired the look of a "tuxedo" kitchen—white cabinets up top and dark cabinets below. We tested out the look on our existing cabinets, painting the tops white and staining the bottoms a darker wood tone. The results aren't bad, but after living with it for a while, we can both agree that it's not the look we want long term.

We're still weighing different countertop options and a slightly tweaked layout (two things that aren't exactly simple to change once you commit), so until we're ready to pull the Phase Two rip cord, we're having fun hunting for inspiration photos, brainstorming new floor plans, and testing out easy and affordable updates to keep the space functional in the meantime.

One of the nicest upgrades we've recently splurged for (thanks to a dishwasher that died on Christmas Day) are new appliances that we can enjoy now and use in our newly renovated kitchen when we finally get there. Oh how we love our shiny new fridge.

On the following pages you'll find real kitchens in various states of completion—some done to the nines and some with just a few small updates while the family saves for a full renovation down the line—as well as tips, tricks, and quick projects for putting your stamp on your own eating space.

Make Your Kitchen Work for You

Kitchens are one of the most hardworking rooms in any house, and different families use them in wildly different ways, so make sure your kitchen meets your family's needs and makes you smile. Sunny and Read's kitchen is a great example of that principle, so here are five elements they used to customize it for their family.

1 EXTRA-TALL BASE CABINETS. Read is 6 foot 4 and Sunny is 5 foot 10, so during the renovation they had a carpenter make the cabinets 5 inches taller than the standard 36-inch height, which is more comfortable for the whole family.

2 AN ANTIQUE ISLAND. They found a secondhand metal table at an antiques mall that was far cheaper than a proper island—plus it's super durable and adds a ton of character.

3 A STAINED WOOD FLOOR. Sunny wanted to work with the existing wood floors while giving them more character, so she applied a two-toned stain pattern using a homemade contact-paper stencil throughout the room, and then sealed it for a durable result. Check out her foyer on page 246 for more details.

(continued)

4 OPEN SHELVING INSTEAD OF A PANTRY.

For Sunny and Read, these casual open shelves turned out to be a more practical and economical solution for their pantry. They use drawers to hide some things away, but having others in plain sight makes food easier to find and use for Sunny. "No more three-year-old pasta buried in the back of a cabinet!" she says.

5 DRAWERS, DRAWERS, AND MORE DRAWERS.

All along one wall, they opted to use big drawer-based cabinets, which they find much easier to organize and access than typical doored cabinets that force you to bend down and root around in the back.

Make a rental your own too.

Cate and Frank wanted to downplay the amount of pine in their rental's kitchen, but painting isn't an option. So they removed the upper cabinet doors and lightly tacked graphic fabric (stretched over lattice strips) to the backs. It created a new, colorful focal point in the room, which is also completely undoable when it's time to reclaim their security deposit!

Turn a **Family Recipe** into Art

Despite being super-functional spaces, the most welcoming and beloved kitchens also have personality and meaning for the people who use them every day. That can seem tricky to accomplish with so many stock choices when it comes to cabinets, countertops, and appliances, but a few special finishing touches can make all the difference.

We hunted down an old handwritten recipe card from John's parents. An all-time favorite snack of his and his sisters' when they were growing up were these Old-Fashioned Butter Cookies, so we paid fifty cents to enlarge the timeworn card at a copy shop (in color so we were sure to capture those charming folds and the old yellowed hue). Then we tossed it into a simple wood frame to pick up on those warm tones.

TIP

Fake it.
If you don't have an old recipe card handy, you can rewrite a favorite recipe on a new index card, and then lightly fold it and tea stain it to create an aged effect.

A Case for **Open Shelves**

We're big fans of open shelves in kitchens, and from the number of houses we've seen them in, we know we're not alone. Open shelves are definitely not for everyone, but here's why they might be an option worth considering.

❉ **THEY'RE EASY TO ACCESS.** Our favorite thing about our shelves is how much easier it is to grab things or put them away. Those few seconds that you save not opening and closing a cabinet door might seem trivial, but we have never unloaded the dishwasher or set the table faster—and we love seeing what we have at a glance.

❉ **THEY LEND LIGHTNESS.** If your kitchen is packed with upper cabinetry and looks heavy and crowded, swapping in some open shelves in one area can make the room feel bigger and less boxy.

❉ **THEY'RE GREAT FOR EVERYDAY ITEMS.** Almost everyone we talk to says they like loading up their open shelves with often-used items that are in constant rotation, so they don't have time to get dusty.

❉ **THEY'RE EASY TO CUSTOMIZE.** Mixing up your storage with some open shelves can add a more varied look to your kitchen—and you can go even further with your choice of shelving materials (sleek white? rustic wood?) and your hanging style (floating? mounted on decorative brackets?). Meg used salvaged wood with sleek Ikea brackets in her kitchen (opposite).

❉ **THEY KEEP YOU "HONEST."** Yes, you do have to maintain a certain amount of order with open shelves, but it's a challenge we appreciate since it encourages us to curate our kitchenware and not own more than we use.

❉ **THE PRICE IS RIGHT.** Open shelves are usually much more affordable than traditional cabinets, which require frames, doors, and hardware (costs that quickly add up), so just using them in one small area can save five hundred dollars or more.

Four Ways to Maximize Your Kitchen

If you're looking to squeeze even more function or organization out of your cooking space, try taking some of these additions for a spin (one literally).

1 FRIDGE LAZY SUSAN. Adding a store-bought lazy Susan to your refrigerator can help all of those shoved-in-the-back items get out in front again (well, with a little spin). Now you won't have to fear what lurks (or stinks) in the dark corners of your fridge.

2 HANGING POT RACK. If your ceiling height allows, consider a rack like Joey and Jeff's. It's one of their favorite and most-used pieces in their kitchen. Joey warns that it might take some practice to get the placement right—you want the pans to hang out of the way of heads, but not so high that they're difficult to access.

3 A SMALL ISLAND. At 24 inches deep and 36 inches long, this island isn't huge, but it adds tons of function—both extra storage and bonus prep surface. So see if you can squeeze one in, even if it's just a rolling cart or a fold-down table.

4 BACKSPLASH SHELVES. These small metal shelves mounted midway up their planked backsplash turn an unused surface into a perfect, quick-access home for items like spices and coffee accessories.

Make the Most of
Your Cabinets

Did deep lower cabinet drawers kill the standard lower cabinet door? We wouldn't go that far, but many people are choosing highly customizable cabinet drawers, which pull out to provide easier access. Check out some of these interesting options.

1 BIG DIVIDED DRAWERS. Emily and Todd chose semi-custom cabinetry for most of their kitchen, but used big drawer bases from Ikea for their island, since they knew its divider system would be perfect for wrangling everything from plates and bowls to Tupperware and trays. Buying the island from Ikea saved the budget and keeps their family of five more organized.

2 SLIDE-OUT PANTRIES. These tall vertical systems take advantage of narrow spaces where a traditional cabinet might swallow items stored all the way in the back. With sliding systems like this one in Anna and Liam's kitchen, you gain access to both sides and it's a lot easier to grab something in the back.

3 PULL-OUT TRASH CANS. Rather than giving up floor space to your refuse and recycling, these add-on options can help tame your trash and keep it out of sight. We used a conversion kit to add pull-out trash cans to one of our existing kitchen cabinets for around thirty-five dollars.

survey says: 41% of the people we polled wish they had a hidden trash can, while 34% already do.

Hook It Up

Let your love of coffee (or tea) out of the closet, er, cabinet. Not only does this easy DIY project put your favorite mugs at your fingertips, it's a graphic and inexpensive way to decorate an empty wall in your kitchen or eating area.

1 Measure and cut a sheet of ¾-inch plywood to fit your wall or mug collection. (We trimmed this one to 33 inches tall and left it 2 feet wide.) We cut our plywood with our table saw at home, but most home-improvement stores can do this for you.

2 Lay the plywood flat and arrange your mugs as they would hang, using a **yardstick** to space them evenly.

3 With a **pencil,** mark the spots where your 1½-inch **cup hooks** should go (double-check the spacing with a yardstick) and pre-drill the holes with an ⅛-inch bit.

4 Prime and paint the board. (We used Sparrow by Benjamin Moore.)

5 Once the board is dry, hand screw the cup hooks into each pre-drilled hole.

6 Nail 2 large **sawtooth hangers** to the back and hang with **anchors** or with **screws** driven into a stud.

Have fun mixing up your mugs. The quirkier the collection, the more interesting the display will be!

Kid-Friendly
Doesn't Mean Sacrificing Good Looks

We visited many homes whose kitchens successfully mixed their family's needs and a high-end look (much like the living rooms we found that strategically combined those two things). And lucky for all of us, it's a little easier to handle messes in spaces with cabinets, counters, and tile. Those surfaces are typically made to withstand spaghetti sauce anyway. There are still a few considerations to make sure little eaters feel welcome in your kitchen and that you don't break out in a sweat when the peanut butter and jelly starts flying.

When Nicole and Jason were building their dream home, they incorporated solutions for their two young kids while keeping in mind that they would be growing up all too quickly.

✳ **A BIG ISLAND.** Rather than dividing square footage to create a breakfast area and a separate island, the family opted to have one central zone where they could all gather. (The oversized island serves as both a prep space and an eating space.)

(continued)

✳ A WIPEABLE BENCH.
Nicole and Jason love the woven stools they found but knew that crumbs would collect in those crannies, so until the kids are older they've added a large, wipeable bench at one end of the island.

✳ A CHANGING TABLE.
With one still in diapers and a third baby on the way, Jason built a temporary changing pad holder on a section of the counter near their mudroom that they don't use for food prep.

Now they're not running upstairs every time someone needs changing. It easily tucks away when they have guests—and once everyone is past the diaper phase, it can be lifted off the counter without leaving a trace.

Designing from Afar

Nicole and Jason
live with
Riley (age 4), Benjamin (age 1), Henri (the dog), and Alphabet (the fish), and they have a new baby on the way
and describe their home as
Unexpected, Uncluttered, and Fun

When Nicole and Jason began construction on their home in Texas, there was one small problem: They still lived in London. They both had a clear vision for the home they wanted but found it difficult to execute it from five thousand miles away. So they hired a local contractor and a decorator who, through lots of e-mails and video chatting, could help them source materials and pull rooms together from afar.

> Might I suggest a doggy door into the fridge?

survey says: "Update the cabinets" was the most popular answer (17%) to "If I could change one thing about my kitchen, I would . . ." (followed by "Update the counters" and "Add more storage," both at 15%).

Make **Seating** Multitask

Chairs or benches in your eating area are obviously a must, but these two ideas prove they can be more than just a place to park your tush.

Hanging Chairs. Folding chairs (left) are great for extra seating in a pinch, but don't feel trapped by basic metal or plastic options. Consider wood versions, which Emily and Shane easily worked into their small kitchen's decor. Now they can seat four people when they have guests without tripping over extra chairs when they don't.

Flip-Top Benches. Built-in seats (opposite) are a great way to give your breakfast area a custom look. Consider options with storage, like the ones Jenny and Jay incorporated. They added stain-proof vinyl cushions to keep things stress-free, and the bench tops fold up for easy access.

We chose a raw wood look for our clothespins, but you can also decoupage, paint, stain, washi tape, or twine-wrap yours for extra interest.

Keep **Clutter** Off Your Counters

Clothespins are a great way to add function in a pinch. (See what we did there? a pinch?) And in your kitchen, they can help keep papers from piling up on your counters. We dressed up this bare kitchen column with a quick and casual fabric-covered organizer. It's a good spot to keep party invitations, concert tickets, gift cards, and other items you don't want to misplace.

1 Cut a **board** to size or have it cut for you at a home-improvement store. (Ours was a 1-by-5-inch board that we cut to be 30 inches long.)

2 Cut your fabric so it's about 2 inches wider than your board on all sides.

3 Spread **Mod Podge** on the front side of the board and carefully place your fabric on top so it's centered with 2 inches of overlap on all sides (pull any wrinkles so it looks nice and flat). Allow the Mod Podge to dry.

4 Flip the board over and add Mod Podge around the back edges, pulling the excess 2 inches of fabric firmly around the back on all sides to be held in place by the Mod Podge. Allow it to dry.

5 Use a strong adhesive like **Super Glue** to affix your clothespins as you'd like. Ours are spaced 10 inches apart (allowing for items to hang below each one, so the top clothespin is closer to the top edge than the bottom one is to the bottom edge).

6 Nail a **sawtooth hanger** onto the back and hang with a **nail**.

The Ol' "Pop of Color"

If a phrase could jump the shark, designers and DIYers like ourselves have probably forced "pop of color" to leap a whole ocean of them. You may have grown tired of the expression, but the idea is still going strong and is perfect to employ in your kitchen. Here's why.

✳ **A LITTLE COLOR IS A GREAT WAY TO DIP YOUR TOE INTO THE WATER.** You can stay in a neutral comfort zone for your big pricey purchases and then add dashes of hue one by one through accessories or other small accents.

✳ **IT CUTS DOWN ON CRAZY.** Too many competing colors can be overwhelming, so using just a few "pops" (they can still be big ones!) can keep a space feeling bold without any sensory overload.

✳ **IT CAN SHAKE THINGS UP.** If a room is feeling too stuffy or boring, try swapping out a piece or two for something in a happy color.

✳ **IT'S LESS EXPENSIVE AND MORE FLEXIBLE.** If you reserve your room's color for small accents, they'll be easier and cheaper to swap out (or repaint) if your tastes change. Heck, you can even make small switches for each season if you're feeling feisty.

✳ **IT GIVES A ROOM A FOCAL POINT.** Our eyes are drawn to color and contrast, so these pops—especially in a neutral room—tell us where to look. This can be helpful if you're trying to draw attention toward (or away from!) something in particular.

✳ **IT'S A SIMPLE FORMULA.** Let's face it, color can be challenging—figuring out what we like, combining colors, finding the right pieces to apply them to. Giving yourself permission to go bold in just a few places makes decorating a little less intimidating—and you're free to add as much or as little as you'd like.

This classic white kitchen needed something special, so these Ballard Designs pendants got a few coats of bold orange spray paint to inject more personality.

Five Other Places to **Add Color**

There are countless ways to add a heaping portion (or just a pinch) of your favorite hue. Here are a handful.

1

1 APPLIANCES. We've all seen colorful laundry appliances, but nonwhite, nonstainless options exist for the kitchen too. Katherine and Richard splurged on a blue range to bring an unexpected moment of color to their classic white kitchen.

2 COOKWARE. Colorful mixing bowls or bright bakeware can happy things up in the kitchen, especially if you have glass cabinets or open shelves.

3 FURNITURE. A colorful breakfast table or the secondhand stools Wendy found are great ways to easily add an accent color.

4 ARTWORK. Find a spot—maybe the blank wall next to the fridge, that space over your stove, or room on an open shelf—to display something bold or bright. Frame your item behind glass so it's more protected from splatters and steam than an exposed canvas.

5 WINDOW TREATMENTS. Roman shades or café curtains can add a nice dose of softness over a sink window, plus they are a great opportunity for layering in color, texture, or pattern.

Expand Your
Kitchen's Footprint

Your kitchen might be smaller and more closed off than you'd like, especially if you live in an older home, but it doesn't always have to stay that way. We closed off a second doorway to gain more counter space in our first house, and we opened a wall to get a lot more light in our second house. So just because a wall or a door is in your space now, well, it doesn't mean it's stuck there for good.

Before

Turn two into one. Aletha and Greg doubled the size of their kitchen by merging an unused and oddly placed office with their midcentury home's formerly narrow kitchen. Their new L-shaped layout brings them so much more storage space—and a nice big island that they use every day.

Dream big. Aletha really wanted a glass-fronted fridge, but it wasn't in their budget. By some miracle, one showed up on Craigslist because it hadn't fit in the seller's kitchen. Aletha got it brand-new and in the box for one-eighth of the cost!

survey says: 56% of the people we polled have wood kitchen cabinets versus 36% whose cabinets are white.

Three Smart Ideas to Steal from This Kitchen

Monica and Dean had some must-haves in mind for their kitchen, but in order for it to stay within their budget, they needed to find savings, too. Here's how they did just that.

1 MIXED CABINETS. The white cabinet finish they wanted was too expensive to use in the whole room, so they saved by choosing their second favorite (a dark stain) and splurged on white for just the island.

2 BORROWED FROM THE BATHROOM. To make use of the dummy drawer front below the sink, they added a bathroom towel bar in the same finish as the rest of the kitchen's hardware. It's both handsome and super functional.

3 SPLURGED SMARTLY. Keeping features like the pot filler that Monica wanted meant compromising elsewhere, so they used affordable subway tile for most of the backsplash and reserved a more expensive marble for an accent over the stove.

Dark Cabinets
Don't Have to Mean a Dark Kitchen

The popularity of bright white kitchens means that lots of white cabinet options exist these days. But white is not the only way to pull off a light and airy cooking space. Emily and Shane adjusted their vision for a white kitchen when they found more affordable solid wood cabinets in a dark finish, which they figured would wear better than the more expensive white alternatives they initially considered. Here are some of the ways they keep the room from feeling heavy.

✳ **USED LIGHT COLORS EVERYWHERE ELSE.** Between the counters, backsplash, pendant lights, and walls, choosing dark cabinets gave them permission to go white just about everywhere else without making the room look too sterile or lacking in drama and contrast.

✳ **BROKE UP THE CABINETRY.** Their small kitchen isn't overwhelmed by cabinetry to begin with, but they broke up the dark surfaces that do exist with features like a white apron sink and some warm wooden shelves.

✳ **WORKED THE LIGHTS AND THE LIGHTING.** With such big windows, Emily and Shane's kitchen is a great candidate for darker cabinetry. And the two big pendant lights over the sink help to keep the room feeling bright even after the sun sets.

survey says: A "walk-in pantry" is the most desired feature for a kitchen, followed by a farmhouse sink and a tile backsplash.

Black and White, and Wood All Over

Natural finishes like the wooden shelves (made from scrap lumber that was left over from Emily and Shane's closet renovation!) help this high-contrast space feel warmer and less harsh.

A Compact Country Kitchen for a Big, Busy Family

Teeni and Trevor
live with
Silas (age 8), Rowan (age 6), twins Sorel and Atley (age 4), and Bandy Blue (the guinea pig)
and describe their home as
Cozy, Homey, and Loved

Teeni and Trevor purchased their 1,200-square-foot 1950s home when she was pregnant with their third child—and then they learned there was a fourth in there too! The kitchen was in rough shape, and with food allergies in the family it was extra important to create a space where meals could be made from scratch. Here's how they squeezed the most out of their tight budget.

1 HOMEMADE COUNTERS. Trevor made the counters from wood project panels they found at a local home-improvement store. They sealed them with a two-part self-leveling epoxy, which kept them affordable and easy to wipe down.

2 OOPS-FRIENDLY FLOORING. "Kid falls and plate drops happen a hundred times a day around here," says Teeni. So instead of tile, they chose softer cork flooring, which Trevor was able to install himself in one day.

"Our kids load the dishwasher and like to cook," Teeni says, "so it's nice to have things at their level so they can help." They keep other items, like knives, mounted out of the way under floating shelves that they built themselves.

survey says: 34% of the people we polled say they cook in their kitchen every day.

A Hidden Island.
To create extra prep space, Teeni and Trevor worked with a local handyman to construct this roll-out island, which tucks beside the dishwasher when it's not in use.

Add a **Casual Island**

We've never actually had one, so we lust after the idea of a fancy kitchen island. And a tropical island. We'll take one of those too. But for those of us without either of them, there are some great alternatives (or in-the-meantime options) for the kitchen, like a rolling cart, an antique buffet, or a steel table.

Industrial Upgrade

Courtney and Jack
live with
Kelly (age 5), Dean (age 3), and Robert (age 3 months)
and describe their home as
Busy, Happy, and Quirky

Courtney and Jack haven't pulled the trigger on their full kitchen remodel yet, but they needed more prep and serving space, so they found an industrial table from a restaurant supply company for a few hundred dollars. It's much cheaper than a traditional island, and they love it so much they plan to incorporate it into their down-the-line kitchen.

This industrial steel table serves all the functions of a tradition island, and it stands up to three energetic kids.

Hey, little girl, do you happen to have any bacon?

survey says: 61% of the people we polled say their kitchen needs renovating.

Where Oh Where to Put the Microwave

The poor microwave. While ranges and refrigerators get all the appliance glory, it seems like we're always trying to minimize the microwave, or at least get it off the counter to free up that precious prep space. So if you're hunting for a place to stash yours, here are four ideas.

1 **BUILT INTO YOUR CABINETRY**
Pro: Perhaps the most polished of options, it helps microwaves look integrated and upscale.

Con: Cabinet-mountable microwaves can cost more and may require frame modifications or added trim for a built-in look.

2 **ON A SHELF**
Pro: A less costly alternative to integrating it into cabinetry, without giving up counter space.

Con: May require a smaller microwave and/or reinforcements to your shelves.

3 **IN A PANTRY**
Pro: Conceals it in a less visible location, meaning you don't need a fancy-looking version.

Con: Steals food storage space, requires an outlet in the pantry, and may require pantry doors to remain open during use (for ventilation).

4 **UNDER YOUR COUNTERS**
Pro: Newer, drawer-style versions make this option more popular and easier to execute.

Con: It's usually more costly and can put your microwave within reach of little hands (although some versions now have a lock code), and you may need to bend down to use it.

survey says: 21% of the people we polled say their kitchen was recently renovated—lucky ducks!

1

2

3

4

Making Everyone Feel at Home

Kevin and Margarete
live with
Trina (age 14), Nick (age 10), and Rufus (the dog)
and describe their home as
Inventive, Active, and Neighborly

Designing a house around a wheelchair-bound family member might feel overwhelming or even budget-breaking to some, but this family has mastered some out-of-the-box thinking to make their home work for all its members, including Kevin and Margarete's ten-year-old son, Nick, who has cerebral palsy.

1 TUB TURNED GARDEN. Nick loves to dig around outside, so Kevin and Margarete turned this Craigslist bathtub into a raised bed that he can easily reach. The sculpture in the center is an old cast left over from one of Nick's surgeries that they painted bright yellow.

2 FUNCTION MEETS MEANING. Removing the vanity base allows Nick to roll right up to the downstairs sink. The wallpaper holds special meaning—it's the same pattern Margarete once had in an apartment in her native Germany. She cleverly covered the part under the sink with clear Plexiglas to protect it from wheelchair scuffs.

3 MOVABLE ISLAND. The once stationary kitchen island made it impossible for Nick to access the kitchen, so Kevin added some heavy-duty caster wheels. Not only can it be rolled out of the way, it also works as a mobile serving surface when the family has company.

Double Duty. The built-in desk in the dining room helps the space function as a work and project zone in addition to an eating spot, which keeps the family together on the first floor more often.

Our **Dining Room** Makeover

The worn periwinkle blue trim and faded floral wallpaper we inherited in our dining room didn't inspire many meals in there, so it became a dumping ground for shopping bags and random craft supplies for way too long. Now—novelty of all novelties!—we have a dining room we can actually dine in. Here's how we inched our way to an "after" that looks and works a lot better for us.

✳ **STRIPPED THE WALLPAPER.** After trying lots of removal techniques (we had five wallpapered rooms to disrobe!) we found that a steamer works best for getting the paper off, while scrubbing with some warm water and vinegar loosens any lingering glue.

Before

(continued)

✳ LIGHTENED THINGS UP.
In addition to spraying the blue trim semigloss white like we did in our living room, we chose a light neutral paint color for the walls (Edgecomb Gray by Benjamin Moore), which we used in our foyer. We love a whole-house paint palette that flows from room to room, so repeating some favorite wall colors in a few different spaces can help tie things together for a less choppy feeling.

✳ WENT BLUE. We found the wooden dining chairs on Craigslist and spray painted them a soft blue tone (Robin's Egg by Rust-Oleum Universal), then added upholstered end chairs from Pier 1.

✳ WENT TO THE CEILING.
The traditional corner built-ins not only got painted, but we removed their scrolly tops and added a header board and new trim to take them all the way to the ceiling, which makes the room feel taller.

✳ SWAPPED TABLES.
Our old 70-inch round table was perfect in our last house but a bit too large for this space, so when we learned that a friend of ours was looking for something similar, we traded tables! Her rectangular one from Crate & Barrel ended up fitting our room better, and it's nice to know that ours is living it up at her house.

✳ MADE ART. We wanted a big piece of art on the back wall, so we cut a large sheet of ¼-inch plywood into a 60-by-42-inch piece (we made a rectangle on the wall with tape to settle on the size). After priming and painting it white for a clean backdrop, we brushed on a variety of leftover paint colors to create something casual and abstract. Some 1-by-2-inch trim helped finish things off (we mitered the corners and secured them with small finish nails). A few sawtooth hangers on the back made it wall-mountable.

A Forgiving Rug

We both grew up with carpeted dining spaces, four kids in the house, and multiple pets, so knowing that dark-toned rugs with lots of movement can hide stains and still look great after decades of use made it easier to shell out for a real Persian rug that should hopefully outlive us all and be virtually indestructible. So far it has endured spaghetti sauce and wine, both of which came up when we gently blotted (while whispering a few prayers under our breath for good measure).

Make Some **Graphic China**

Hanging plates on the wall has long been a trick for decorating kitchens or dining spaces, primarily using decorative dishware or vintage platters to complement traditional decor. But you can put a more modern, graphic twist on the same concept with some painter's tape and spray paint.

1 Determine your plate arrangement on a flat surface. We went with a traditional symmetrical grouping of **thrift-store plates** to contrast with the modern designs we'd be adding.

2 Use **painter's tape** to cover areas of the plates, carefully creating stripes, triangles, and any other shapes you'd like. Use **scissors** to cut clean edges wherever needed. Press the edges of the tape firmly to avoid bleeding.

3 On a **drop cloth,** spray your plates a range of colors. We used Rust-Oleum Gloss Protective Enamel in Navy, Sunburst Yellow, and Maui Blue.

4 Once the plates are dry, remove the tape. If any paint bled (especially near the curves in the plate), use a fingernail or a dull knife to scrape it off.

5 Flip your plates over and use **heavy-duty glue** to adhere **sawtooth hangers** to the back of each one. This will determine how the plate hangs, so make sure your pattern is oriented the way you want it to be when you glue the hanger to the back. (You can also use plate hangers, but they will be visible from the front.)

Mix Materials, Styles, and Price Ranges

We love a mix when it comes to dining chairs and tables, rather than a matching set purchased all at once. A little chair/table variety brings interest and personality to a room—and it might just save you a little money too.

Keep it kid-friendly. Courtney and Jack found that embracing a style mix gave them permission to pick mess-resistant chairs in their primary eating space. The modern West Elm chairs add a splash of color, while the translucent ghost chairs (scored on Amazon) help tie in the home's existing crystal chandelier.

Save on your must-haves. Carrie knew she wanted a big dining table that could handle large craft parties, so when she and Matt fell in love with a long mixed-finish option from Restoration Hardware, they waited for a coupon to come around. Then they also saved big on some contrasting modern chairs by finding assemble-yourself versions online.

survey says: 54% of the people we polled prefer to keep their dining room feeling more casual than formal.

Formal Doesn't Mean Off-Limits

Dining rooms, especially when you have another spot for casual eating, can be a great place to crank up the fancy factor without sacrificing livability.

1 WASH IT. Using slipcovered chairs is a great way to avoid worrying about your dining room. Nicole and Jason used washable outdoor fabric for the slipcovers on their dining chairs, which has even stood up to a grape jelly explosion! Katherine and Richard also opted for easy-wash slipcovers in their dining room, which doubles as a homework zone and gift-wrapping command center.

2 WEATHER IT. Rustic or already-worn items not only add great texture but also can be blissfully stress-free when compared to something pristine. Nicole and Jason just shrug off any light wear or wine stains, which blend into their reclaimed wood table's already character-filled surface.

3 WALLPAPER IT. Dining rooms are a great candidate for wallpaper. You can luxe things up without having to worry about moisture like you might in a steamy kitchen or bathroom. If you're nervous about little hands grubbing it up, metallic paper also works well on the ceiling.

Did someone say formal? I'll get my top hat.

survey says: One-third of the people we polled say they use their dining room a few times a year or less.

Don't Waste an **Illuminating** Opportunity

If you love dramatic, oversized, or showstopping light fixtures (we do!), the dining room is your chance to live it up. Not only do these rooms often call for interesting and ornate fixtures, they're also likely to have the space to go grander than you can in rooms where you need clearance to walk under the light fixture (says the family who bemoans their standard 8-foot ceilings). Here, Jenny and Jay had fun layering a sculptural oversized light into their colorful dining room.

How Much Light Do I Need?

A very general rule of thumb is to take the square footage of the room (the length times the width) and multiply it by 1.5, which reveals a ballpark wattage number. So a 10-by-12-foot dining room (120 square feet) would call for 180 watts, or three 60-watt bulbs. Although most CFL and LED bulbs show wattage equivalents, it's not always an exact science when it comes to comparing the actual light output (which is measured in lumens). So if your head is spinning, try this instead: overcompensate with a fixture that accommodates more bulbs than you need and install a dimmer switch to adjust as desired (bright for daily mealtimes and subdued for cozy dinners).

SLEEPING SPACES

John says

IN SOME CASES (like when you're growing up or sharing an apartment with roommates), bedrooms are the be-all-end-all room that you get to call your own, acting as your sleeping/working/ playing/living room. But at some point you may have a home where you have other rooms to use for those purposes, so a bedroom doesn't need to be much more than a bed in a room. Okay, and maybe a spot for your clothes.

The funny thing is that if your bedroom is big, it can actually end up being a multifunctional room again. You might have space in it for a chair in the corner, a TV, or even a desk. We saw a model home once with a coffee bar and a mini-fridge in a walk-in closet, practically making that bedroom a fully functional house on its own.

The range of bedroom functions is actually less fascinating to me than the journey we take with our bedrooms throughout our lives. When we were little kids, they might've been home to our toys and games and a mountain of stuffed animals—a comfortable space where sleep was almost secondary. When we were teens, our bedrooms became a canvas for self-expression—a refuge where we could plaster whatever posters we liked on the walls. And then somewhere in our adult life the bedroom became very serious for us—like "We're grown-ups; we need to rest now"—and it skewed more toward a hotel room, and less toward *our* room.

I'm not saying this is necessarily a bad thing, because having a calm retreat from the nuttiness of the rest of your day can be great. But when Sherry and I looked at how fun we made our kids' bedrooms, sometimes ours felt meh by comparison.

Our first home's bedroom had a very soft color palette and framed photos of sunsets that we took ourselves (not joking here). It was actually featured on an HGTV show under the description "spa-like retreat." Our second bedroom was still pretty muted color-wise, though we went with darker paint and furnishings to give it a cozier feel. It wasn't until we moved into our current house that something struck us when we were standing

Here's the "spa-like retreat" we created in our first house.

there staring at our bedroom in its blank-slate state. Why were we being so restrained in our former bedrooms? We loved them, and they certainly felt restful and calm; but in hindsight, they lacked a lot of the personality that we take so much joy injecting into almost every other room of our house.

So we set out to have a little more fun this time, putting a richer color on the walls, a cheerful rug on the floor, and (our favorite part) a collage of family photos fanning out around our homemade headboard. It's not the most traditional choice for a bedroom, but it's our way of putting our personal stamp on the room so it feels 100 percent like us. Now instead of the room feeling light and calm, the deep color makes it feel cozy and the family photos make it feel happy, which turns out to be a pretty good combo for us.

Thin wood frames with big white mats help to unify a large collection of colorful photos.

Our **Guest Room** Makeover

We feel very lucky to have a spare bedroom to host guests, but it has long been the room that held our mismatched "furniture leftovers," so we thought a little update was in order. Here's what we added.

✳ **A DEEP WALL COLOR.** With three big windows, this room gets tons of natural light, but since it's a space that's primarily meant for sleeping, we wanted it to feel cozy too. A rich chocolate color (Sparrow by Benjamin Moore) does just that and sets the stage for some lighter accents.

✳ **A CURVACEOUS HEADBOARD.** We scored this baby on Craigslist for $40, but we didn't love its pink whitewashed finish or wicker panels. Thankfully, the back had a nice clean wicker-less look, so we bought it, primed it, painted it white, and turned it around. You'd never know it's not the front!

✳ **MOUNTED LIGHTING.** We knew nightstands on both sides of the bed would be a great functional addition, but chunky lamps wouldn't fit easily. Enter these wall-mounted sconces, stage right. They're of the plug-in variety (no new wiring needed!), plus we bought them for half off at a local lighting outlet.

✳ **CURTAINS AND CROWN.** To bring more polish to the room, we installed crown molding to match the rest of our bedrooms. (We hired someone to do this task in our first home, but we learned how to do it for our second and third houses.) And finding four posh linen-looking curtain panels at HomeGoods allowed us to double up on each side of the window wall for a fuller look.

Before

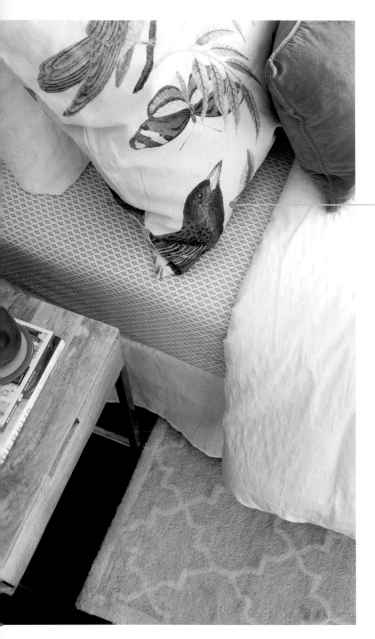

Bring some personality to white bedding.

We always gravitate toward crisp white bedding, but to keep the guest room from feeling too stark, we added color and charm with some patterned sheets and bold shams from Pottery Barn that keep the room from taking itself too seriously. When in doubt, put a bird on it!

Mix materials.

These Target nightstands were a great find, not only because of their size (they fit perfectly on each side of the bed). Their wood tops and steel bases tie in the wood accent mirror over the bed and the polished nickel sconces. It's awesome to find those "bridge pieces" that can marry a mix of materials.

A Simple Formula for a **No-Fuss Bedroom**

Lucky for us grown-ups, our bedrooms don't usually need to be nearly as multifunctional as our kids' rooms do. In most cases, as long as we've got a spot to rest our heads at night, and a closet or dresser for our clothes, it can be considered a successful bedroom. So if you're struggling to update your sleeping space, think about it in simple terms and stop stressing. Try starting with the following and then expand based on your needs.

1 **LAMP.** Here's a good place to add a little personality, since chic lighting can be found affordably online, in local boutiques or outlets, and in big-box stores. Just make sure the lampshade isn't wider than your nightstand or it can look top-heavy.

2 **ACCENT WALL.** If you're struggling with what to hang over your bed (mirror? art? photo of your cat?), try creating an accent wall via paint, wallpaper, a stencil, or even some trimwork (a grid-like pattern in a glossy white, tan, or charcoal color, for example). It will help the room feel more finished, plus it's a great spot to bring in a pattern—even a subtle one.

3 **HEADBOARD.** It's the quickest way to make your bed—and the whole room—look more finished. Something simple, like an upholstered rectangular headboard, will add easy polish. You can branch out by using tufting, trim, or a curvier or more geometric shape.

survey says: Three is the most common number of bedrooms in the homes of the people we polled (42%).

4 NIGHTSTAND. A simple spot to place a lamp and corral your nighttime necessities (books, contact lens case, diary of all your prophetic dreams) should do the trick. Try to get something level with or slightly higher than your mattress, since something too low can look odd and be harder to reach.

5 BEDDING. While all kinds of patterns and colors can be fun, crisp white duvet covers are a pretty foolproof choice. There's a reason hotels use them so much (they're bleachable, clean-looking, and classic). And then you can add patterned pillows, sheets, or coverlets.

6 RUG. Even if you have wall-to-wall carpet, layering in an area rug that runs beneath your bed can help define the sleeping area while providing an extra-soft spot for your feet to land each morning.

Go bold!
Nightstands are a nice place to inject some color into your bedroom. If you can't find a colorful option in the store, it's a pretty low-risk item to paint yourself—especially if you can find one at a thrift store or on Craigslist.

Make a **Dreamy** Blurred Stripe **Headboard**

Headboards are one of the best ways to make a basic mattress set look less like a, you guessed it, basic mattress set. And many types—like fabric-covered, painted, or stained wood—are easy to make yourself. So if you have a bedroom that's lacking in the headboard department, here's one way to remedy that.

1 Cut a sheet of smooth ¼-inch plywood (at the store or at home) to fit the width of your bed and the height you would like. (Our full-sized bed was 54 inches wide and we chose 24 inches for the height.)

2 Use a **yardstick** and a **pencil** to mark 2-inch increments on all sides of the plywood.

3 Apply strips of 1½-inch-wide **painter's tape** diagonally across the board, using the 2-inch marks as your guide.

4 Press each strip of tape down firmly, especially along the edges, to keep stain from seeping under them too much (it will a bit for a blurry effect).

5 Outside on a **drop cloth** or other work surface, use a **paintbrush** or a rag to apply a thin coat of **stain** across the wood. We used Minwax's Dark Walnut.

6 Allow to dry, following the directions on the jar or can, then wipe off any excess stain with a **rag** or a paper towel.

(continued)

5

6

7 After about eight hours, carefully remove the tape. The edges will be imperfect because the wood grain soaks up the stain beneath the tape slightly, creating that dreamy blur.

8 Brush on a coat or two of **clear polyurethane sealer** for protection. (You can use one in a matte finish if you want to maintain the raw look of the wood.)

9 To frame your headboard like we did, cut 1-by-2-inch pieces of wood to the appropriate lengths for each side. (You may want to skip the bottom side so that the mattress is more flush to the headboard.) Attach the pieces with wood glue and nails, leaving a small lip on the back side if possible.

10 Hang the headboard on the wall by resting the back lip of the frame on **screws** in studs or heavy-duty anchors. Make sure the bottom edge sits slightly below the top of your mattress for a seamless look.

survey says: 60% of the people we polled sleep on a queen-sized bed, while 30% sleep on a king.

Use Every **Inch**

Adding built-in clothing storage between corner
closets in Sunny and Read's room not only
compensated for limited closet space, it also
created a feature wall in their bedroom, complete
with a vanity area and extra book storage.

Nightstand Notes

Your bedside table doesn't have to come from the nightstand aisle. You'll find more options and a better fit for your space if you consider side tables, dressers, desks, and even entry consoles. As well as adding character, a non-nightstand piece may provide bonus functions—like extra clothing storage or a desk-like area to write letters. Just be sure to know your bed's height while hunting (so you can aim for things that are in the same ballpark).

Repurpose.
When Abby and Tait were furnishing their vacation home, this old narrow table worked perfectly as a casual night table.

Keep your whites white.
Abby and Tait stock their vacation home with only white linens since it simplifies the laundry process. Abby's tip for keeping them bright white isn't bleach, but line-drying them in the sun whenever possible.

Mount your light.
If space for a nightstand is small or nonexistent, put your reading light up on the wall. Sunny and Read mounted sconces to free up room for books and other nighttime needs.

Rescue a hand-me-down.
No one in Sunny's family wanted this inherited dresser because of a bad faux-wood finish, but some high-gloss blue paint made it much more her style and now she loves it by her bedside.

Build-In Your Bed

A great way to add coziness to a bedroom is to nestle the bed into a shallow nook, whether it's part of the room's architecture or something you create with bookshelves or wardrobes on either side. This kind of customization not only gives you a lot of added storage, function, and display space, it can also up the room's charm and give your sleeping spot that cozy, nestled feel.

1 MIX MATERIALS. A combination of wood shelves and clean white walls feels warm yet crisp in Lisa and Mike's room. Varying the materials and finishes in your room can add interest and make things feel extra custom.

2 TRY A NIGHTSTAND ALTERNATIVE. When Lisa and Mike had their built-ins made, they included cubbies on each side that could be accessed from the bed. These small nooks can hold books and other nightstand staples, plus each one has an outlet for charging devices along with a switch that operates the sconces.

3 INCORPORATE PERSONAL ART. Lisa and Mike kept the shelves simple and meaningful, which is a great approach in a private space. We love the addition of this drawing their young son made to cheer on the family's favorite football team.

I sleep on my dad's head. How's that for cozy?

survey says: 80% of the people we polled prefer their bedrooms to be light and airy, versus wanting a dark and cozy vibe.

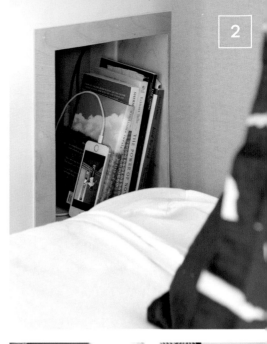

A Maximized One-Bedroom Apartment

Kai
lives with
Eli (age 3), Oliver (age 3), and Pilot (the dog)
and describes her home as
Eclectic, Colorful, and Comfortable

After months of looking for something that fit her budget, her commute, and the life she wanted for herself, her twin boys, and their dog, Kai didn't expect a 700-square-foot one-bedroom apartment to speak to her. But it felt so right that she convinced the landlord she could make it work. ("At first I got denied because on the outside, a single mom and two kids in a one-bedroom sounds ridiculous.") And make it work she did. "I've never had to work harder on my organizational and decluttering skills, but we all love it here."

Dividing and Conquering

Kai's three-year-old twins, Eli and Oliver, share the apartment's single bedroom, so Kai adapted the main living space as if it were a studio apartment. One side became their living area, complete with a sofa and TV, and on the opposite wall, her bedroom area is defined by a large piece of art. Her bed functions like a daybed during the day, and her nightstand doubles as a desk.

Temporary Kid Art

Kai took pages from a French Superman comic book, Mod Podged them to foam core, and hung them with poster tape. They're 100 percent removable and won't hurt the walls.

Defined Dining

The open area between the bed and the couch works as a dining space, and the table has a built-in leaf if they need to expand the eating space. The arc lamp is the perfect rental substitute for a hardwired light fixture.

Seeing Double

Kai purchased one of these red twin beds for herself after her separation. When the boys outgrew their cribs, she bought another and upgraded herself to a full-sized bed. The red not only adds lots of fun against the rental's white walls but also ties in nicely with the colorful art found on Craigslist.

Mirror Play

Mirrors are great surfaces to have fun with, especially since the face of them is smooth enough to redo whenever the mood strikes. You can casually tape photos up with washi tape around the edges, doodle around with a dry-erase marker, or add some pattern with vinyl, like we did here.

1 Unroll a section of **vinyl** (we used a roll intended for craft cutters from Jo-Ann Fabric and Crafts) on top of your **cutting surface** and mark lines of varying thicknesses using your ruler and pencil. We did 1-inch-, ¾-inch-, and ½-inch-wide pieces.

2 Use your **craft knife** to cut strips of vinyl, relying on your **ruler** as a straightedge.

3 Peel the backing off of one piece at a time, starting with the thickest strip, and place it diagonally in the corner of your mirror. We just eyeballed it. (The vinyl is forgiving enough that it can be easily removed and repositioned; it can also be recut and reapplied if it gets wrinkled when you pull it off.) Don't worry about the excess in the corners; you'll cut that off in a second.

4 Place the other strips. If you're mimicking our pattern, put more space between them as you move away from the corner.

5 With each strip pressed firmly into place, carefully run your blade along the inner edge of the mirror to trim off any excess vinyl.

6 If you ever tire of the pattern, the vinyl can be peeled off easily and any remaining residue can be removed with soap and water.

Don't Feel Trapped by **Closet Doors**

You may be able to make your closet work harder for you just by rethinking the doors. Here are two wildly different ways to do just that.

Take 'em off.

If your closet offers you more with the doors off, we say go for it! In fifteen-year-old Kippy's room, her mom added a thrift-store vanity to one of her doorless double closets, which creates an area where Kippy gets ready for school each morning.

Fill 'em up.

Seventeen-year-old Presley wanted a big pinboard in her room, so she and her mom covered two door-sized pieces of Homasote board with fabric and screwed them right into the front of her flat-panel doors. Adding leather handles they found online dresses things up and keeps it easy to access everything inside.

Heart Art

Megan and Greg like to commemorate each place they've been stationed through DIY art, as well as other collected items they place throughout their home.

Tips from a Military Wife for Sprucing Up a Rental Home

Megan and Greg
live with
Henry (age 3)
and describe their home as
Fresh, Colorful, and Modern

Megan's husband, Greg, is a U.S. Marine, and they're currently living in their fifth house in nine years. So not only are they moving pros, but she's quite well versed when it comes to turning temporary residences into homey spaces (even if just for a little while).

"We love living on base, but in most military housing communities, every single home in a neighborhood is identical to the next, from the floor plan and finishes to wall colors and landscaping. We've learned that with some budget-friendly ingenuity, it is possible to create spaces that truly look and feel like 'home' no matter where or how far away the military may send us!" Here are her top tips for making your mark on a home that you may not be in for very long.

✳ **Take advantage of what's yours.** If painting walls is off-limits, infuse some major personality into a space with items that come with you when you move, like colorful textiles and accessories. You could literally take everything out of one house and set it up in your next home without having to lift a paintbrush!

✳ **Give it a temporary twist.** In military housing, you have to leave the house in the exact condition you found it, so anything and everything you do has to be removable or reversible. This kitchen backsplash is fully removable; it's made with vinyl rectangles applied in a crosshatch pattern.

✳ **Change what you can.** Knocking down walls, painting cabinets, and changing flooring is typically not allowed in rentals. Instead try swapping out light fixtures, removing unsightly window blinds, and laying rugs over beat-up carpeting—all things you can undo before moving out. Little details like these will separate your house from all the others just like it and give you that much-desired sense of ownership when you walk in the door.

✳ **Embrace it.** Use frequent moves as an opportunity to determine what you like and experiment with designs before committing to them in your "forever home." Don't hesitate to try a bold color or a new window treatment. In just a few years it will all come down, and you don't have to replicate it at the next house if you don't want to.

Teddy's Worldly
Closet Wall

No space is too small for a little personality. As with our daughter's closet, shown on page 290, we wanted our son's to double as a hidden play space (since we have tons of clothing storage in his room). From the moment we spotted a charming book called *Maps* by Aleksandra Mizielinska and Daniel Mizielinski, we knew it would add up to an awesome closet upgrade for our little cartographer-in-training.

1 You'll need enough **paper/pages** to cover your back wall. If dismantling a book isn't your speed, try sheet music, kid art, or to-be-completed word searches and crossword puzzles.

2 Prep your wall by wiping off dust or grime with a **damp cloth**.

3 Carefully remove your book pages. Pages from books with glued bindings may pull free with a slow, firm tug. You can also run a sharp **craft knife** along the inside seam to free the pages.

4 Lay your page facedown on a large scrap piece of **cardboard** and use a **paintbrush** to apply a thorough coat of **wallpaper paste** to the back (any part left dry may cause bubbles to form). We used DIF Universal Wallcovering & Border Adhesive and coated the wall too (with both surfaces slicked up, it was easier to slide each page into place).

5 A wallpaper smoother wasn't necessary in our case, but a credit card can work well if you find that you need a tool to smooth the surface (we just smoothed by hand).

6 Repeat these steps, adding one page at a time until the wall is covered. When you reach an edge, dry fit the paper by pushing the unpasted page into the corner to make a crease and use a craft knife to cut off the excess before applying paste and adhering it.

Involving Your Kids in Their Bedroom's Design

The moment Clara was old enough to express interest in how her room looked was exciting for us because we want that space to be something she loves and feels ownership of. She was proud to be asked for input, but we also knew our role as parents was to guide her wishes, wants, and wacky suggestions in the direction of functional and realistic ideas that we could all get behind. (She once requested a toilet and sink in the corner of her room. . . .) Obviously every child and every age is different, but here are a few things to think about when you're asking for his or her preferences.

When Kippy outgrew the bubble-gum-pink walls in her bedroom, she had a clear vision for her teenage room: a bed with a white headboard and a colorful bedspread placed on an accent wall. Her mom, Amy, jumped right in and helped make Kippy's vision a reality, which even included learning how to hang wallpaper. (See page 207 for some wallpaper hanging tips.)

✳ **START WITH QUESTIONS ABOUT THE FEEL OF THE ROOM,** not the look. Focus on the big picture first with questions like, "Do you want your room to feel cozy? happy? fancy? outdoorsy?" This can help get you and your child on the same page before talking details. And going into the process with a vibe in mind can help with specific choices. ("If you want a cozy camping feeling, maybe wood on the walls with plaid sheets would be fun—what do you think?")

(continued)

Hooray for Homemade Art

Jessica's seven-year-old daughter, Reese, loves lots of colors, so her aunt Robin bought a big canvas and let Reese paint in all of her favorite hues. The result is a piece of art that brings personality to the room and can stay with Reese as she grows.

✳ **OFFER THEM CHOICES.**
A great way to let your child feel involved without having free rein (which might result in all-black walls or requests for furniture that's not within the budget) is to present options for them to choose from. For example, find three bedspreads in your price range that you think could work and let your child have the final say. She gets the thrill of making the choice, while you don't have to sweat about it.

✳ **GIVE THEM COMPLETE POWER SOMEWHERE.**
If your child suggests something impractical or budget-busting and you feel like you've been party pooping the design process too much, try finding a place where you can let your child loose—and be willing to bite your tongue. For example, tell her she can paint her closet door any color she wants, or that she can hang whatever art she wants over the bed.

Shake Up Your Stenciling

We've long been fans of stencils as a great (and not super-costly or permanent) way to add pattern to your walls. To achieve this effect, we broke out not one, not two, but *four* different paint rollers for a colorful striped twist on our usual stencil MO.

1 Choose your **stencil** and color palette. We went with a Neapolitan ice cream–inspired scheme—Benjamin Moore's Sylvan Mist, Proposal, Ashen Tan, and Nelson Blue—and used the Large Primitivo Lace stencil from Royal Design Studio (which already had rows of different shapes within the one stencil).

2 If you're using four different colors, you'll need **four small foam rollers** and **four roller trays,** each filled with one of the colors.

3 Our pattern has no discernible "center," so we started in one corner and worked across, but if yours does, begin in the center of your wall and work your way out.

4 Use a **level** to ensure that your stencil is straight or that it sits flush with your baseboard or crown molding, then hold it in place with **painter's tape.**

5 Get paint on your first roller and use the paint tray to remove any excess. For the best results, you only want to apply a light coating of paint every time you roll it on the wall.

6 Use one hand to help hold the stencil against the wall as you lightly roll on your first color, being careful to cover only the area of the stencil that you want to be that color. (In other words: Stay in your lane if you're doing stripes.)

7 Repeat with all the other colors until you have gone over the entire stencil.

(continued)

8 Carefully remove your stencil and gently wipe or dab the back side with a **paper towel** or a rag to remove any excess paint that seeped around. This will help you keep your wall clean as you place the stencil the next time.

9 Use the registration marks on the stencil to carefully line it up with the portion you just painted. If no registration marks exist, consider slightly overlapping the stencil with the painted portion to ensure proper placement.

10 Repeat steps 6 through 9 until your wall is complete. And get ready to have lots of people pawing your wall and saying, "I thought this was wallpaper!"

Tape It Up

Kids seem to change their minds faster than they can text, so an easy-to-update art grid won't have you making holes every time there's a new Instagram picture to hang or another friend getting promoted to bestie status. Washi tape makes this simple and adds some extra color and pattern to the arrangement.

Ditch **DIY** for **DIT** (Do It Together)

Another great way to get your kids involved in their room decor is to let them get their hands dirty, assuming your child is old enough to lend a hand. For Benjamin's tween room, he and his mom, Katja, worked on over a dozen DIYs—making everything from the pillows to the gallery wall, which was inspired by an art class they took together. Their favorite joint project was creating the pixelated Mario art next to the bed.

Making Mario

Benjamin came up with the idea to "do something pixilated," so Katja helped him map out a grid to see how many squares of each color they would need. They cut their squares from thick pieces of card stock, which were around 2 inches wide, to create a 5-foot Mario after applying them to the wall with foam tape.

Crouching Tiger, Hidden Mattress

Katja and Frank customized an Ikea trundle bed to roll under Benjamin's bed, which helps them accommodate more visiting relatives and friends.

Let It **Gooooo**

Perfection is overrated, and it can be pretty futile to chase the idea of a bedroom always having perfectly fluffed bedding and a clean, clear floor, especially in a kid's room. So it can be incredibly freeing (and a lot more fun for the kids) if you embrace a little lived-in imperfection. Sometimes things like charmingly mixed patterns and art that's casually taped on the walls can make the room feel a lot more homey anyway. Here are two more ways to worry even less.

1 THINK SECONDHAND.
Kids' rooms are a great place to incorporate thrift-store finds and hand-me-down pieces. You'll appreciate not having to spend full price for everything, plus it's a chance to bring in interesting pieces that will give the room a more collected-over-time feel.

2 WOOD WALLS CAN TAKE A BEATING.
Consider slatted wood for rooms that see lots of activity—whether as wainscoting or a whole accent wall—since it's a durable material that also adds character. Joey and Jeff found reclaimed wood for the bottom portion of their daughter's room, but chose inexpensive pine for the rest since they knew they were going to paint it.

This is the moment that inspired the room! Nick asked *Parks and Rec* star Nick Offerman, "Would it be weird if you took a picture with my baby?" He replied, "Son, life is weird."

An Unusually Themed but Not Themey Nursery

Amber and Nick
live with
Ramona (age 5) and Beckett (age 1)
and describe their home as
Unexpected, Storied, and Playful

When doing their son Beckett's nursery, Amber and Nick found a theme in a pretty unusual place: a charity barbecue competition. There they met celebrity guest judge Nick Offerman, known for playing comically outdoorsy and carnivorous Ron Swanson on the show *Parks and Recreation*. Beckett was there for the momentous meeting (meating?) and thus the direction for their son's room was born.

"We're not really into 'theme rooms,' so it's more of a mood we were going for. We wanted a rustic, woodsy feel," said Amber.

The star of the space (besides Beckett, of course) is the mountainous wall mural that they created using layers of paint and painter's tape. Nick sketched out the random-ish pattern and carefully placed the tape using a ruler and a level.

Amber and Nick tried to keep their budget and timeline to a minimum, so they used lots of affordable items like an Ikea crib and a fifteen-dollar Urban Outfitters rug along with pieces they already had, like their cool secondhand midcentury dresser.

Nods to the "theme" are added with a soft touch: the mountain-range mural, the flannel changing-pad cover, and lots of wood pieces. The only clue that Ron Swanson was the launch point for the design is the commemorative poster from the event that hangs on the wall.

Make Use of
the Ceiling

In rooms with low ceilings, you're sometimes inclined to deflect attention from them when, in fact, they can be utilized to draw the eye up and make the space feel taller. You can simply paint the ceiling an accent color (try a lighter shade than the walls, for instance) or even apply a subtle pattern via wallpaper or a stencil. Six-year-old Towne's mom, Christi, gave her room a sense of height and drama by hanging curtain rods along the ceiling and then draping fabric panels at each corner, creating a soft and cozy four-poster-bed look.

Christi also made the room feel lighter and less cluttered by hanging an egg chair from the ceiling, visually (and literally) freeing up floor space.

Letter Rip

Decorating with letters is one of the quickest ways to put a personal stamp on a room. And with craft stores selling tons of varieties (not to mention what you'll find in thrift shops or online), the options are endless for further customizing your most treasured member of the alphabet. Here are four ideas, which can be used for single initials (we like hanging one on each of our children's doors) or for mixing and matching to create your favorite word.

✳ **YARNED.** A gradient effect was made by simply wrapping multicolored yarn tightly around a cardboard *L* we got from Jo-Ann Fabric and Crafts. The yarn was secured at the beginning and end with a flat tack in the back. Try painting the letter beforehand with a coordinating color (ours is secretly magenta) so any gaps in the yarn don't look unfinished.

✳ **FRINGED.** After painting a cardboard *O* white, we hot-glued some pink pom-pom fringe around the outside for a little added fun.

✳ **GLITTERED.** A cardboard *V* got the white paint treatment before being coated with Mod Podge. Then a dusting of fine white glitter up top and some deeper gold glitter on the bottom gave it a sparkly two-toned look.

✳ **DECOUPAGED.** We broke out the Mod Podge again to adhere playful fabric to a navy-painted cardboard *E*. We applied it just to the front (Mod Podging the face of the letter, pressing the fabric down on it, and trimming the excess so the navy sides would show). You can touch up any fraying on the fabric edges with another coat of Mod Podge.

WASHING SPACES

John says

WE'VE ALREADY COVERED that room where you wash your dishes (I'm gonna go out on a limb here and assume most people do that in their kitchen), so this chapter is really about where you wash your, um, *self* (the bathroom) and your clothes (the laundry room). They're rooms in your house that can pack a lot of function into a little space and can make your home life a lot more convenient (this is coming from two former Manhattanites who still have flashbacks of dragging a bag of laundry down the street to the Laundromat).

Washing spaces are also some of our favorite rooms to update, whether we're doing quick aesthetic improvements or totally gutting a room to the studs. Their relatively small footprints can help you limit the amount of money, time, and effort you'll have to spend, no matter how far you want to crank up the makeover dial.

Take the upstairs hall bathroom in our current house, which is used by our kids and occasional overnight guests. We recently gave it some purely cosmetic love by painting the walls and brown vanity base a crisp white, which took the old yellow floor tiles from dated to cheerful (yellow + brown can look like a fast-food restaurant, but yellow + white looks so fresh and happy). We also swapped out the builder-basic mirrors and the old lights along with adding colorful art, new hand towels, and gleaming cabinet knobs.

When the DIY dust cleared, a long weekend's worth of work made the old tile look downright charming, cost less than $250, and staved off the urge for a much more major overhaul—although we're still itching to switch out those faucets, and would eventually love to upgrade the counter.

Picture us turning the imaginary home-improvement dial up a notch when it came to our half bathroom downstairs, where a space-hogging vanity and an old toilet just weren't working for us. We replaced them both with more efficient and eye-pleasing options, along with adding crown molding, repainting the once-wallpapered walls, and switching out the mirror, all of which you'll see in a lot more detail when you turn the page.

And we pretty much cranked the ol' DIY dial all the way to "extreme" when it came to our laundry space. After living in two previous homes where the laundry area was more of a closet or hallway situation that greeted us at our back door, we were psyched when the opportunity presented itself to create a legit laundry room, with four walls and an actual door!

What that meant was transforming a cramped and dark laundry closet at the end of an upstairs hallway into a much larger laundry room by moving walls and plumbing lines and basically building the space from scratch. But oh, was it worth it. We were left with a *bona fide room* that wasn't there before—complete with new cabinets, shelving, countertops, tile flooring, a drying/sorting area, and a proper door that we can close to muffle the sound of laundry in progress. Plus we got to try out some design choices (like a gleaming marble backsplash) and DIY skills (like installing under-cabinet lighting), both of which could come in handy in our eventual kitchen renovation.

Lest you think we have it all figured out, remember that we still need to renovate our master bathroom, but there are a bunch of ideas in this chapter that have us pretty excited about that challenge.

Before

Our **Half Bathroom** Makeover

The small half bathroom on our first floor started out with dark wallpaper, blue trim, and a surprisingly tiny vanity mirror. (Maybe we just have big faces?) We stripped the walls and painted everything white to tide us over for a while, and when we were finally ready to fully redo the space, we used the room's small size as an excuse to splurge on a few beyond-basic fixtures and features that made all the difference.

Before

✳ **A LEGGY NEW SINK.** We wanted a less boxy sink base to make this small room feel more spacious. (Did we mention that the former setup boasted an almond-colored seashell-shaped sink?) The old vanity's cabinets had been empty since we moved in, so first we considered a pedestal sink. Then we saw a sink with ceramic legs in a catalog and, well, it was love. We learned that they're called "console sinks," and although many that we hunted down were over a thousand dollars, we managed to buy this Nottingham sink for $350 from a discount site called Signature Hardware. It's 30 inches wide with ample counter space, and a basket of toilet paper can still live happily underneath it, along with a handy blue stool for Clara.

(continued)

✳ MIRROR, MIRROR. We yearned for this sculptural mirror from Ballard Designs forever, but it was sold out (cue the dramatic music). When it came back into stock in a new size that was perfect for our bathroom (cue the angelic choir), we took it as a sign that it was meant to be and grabbed it during a 20-percent-off holiday sale. The rounded edges look great with our curvy sink, and it's large enough for us to see our big faces without any of the where'd-the-top-of-my-head-go issues that we previously had.

✳ A NEW THRONE. The last few years have marked a new phase for us: toilet coveting. We didn't want anything with ambient music or mood lighting, but a clean-lined look that's more comfortable and has better flushing power certainly was compelling. To get over our sticker shock, we kept an eye out for sales and eventually scored this Kohler Memoirs model during a holiday promotion. It still cost a bit more than the basic models we used to buy, but we got it for less than half of its MSRP, and we love it more than two people should ever love a toilet.

✳ PEARLY WALLS. The walls are the same sandy gray as the adjacent foyer, but we wanted to add a hint of interest. So we gave them one thin coat of Pearlescent White Metallic Glaze by Benjamin Moore. Using a small foam roller, we carefully applied it one wall at a time in long vertical strokes, being sure not to roll over areas that started to dry. The result? A soft sheen that adds a little luxe to the space.

Go for Some Amazing **Lace**

When we spotted this charming little table at a thrift store, we thought it'd be great for breaking up an otherwise crisp white bathroom. The curved legs were calling out for a bit of romance in the form of a lace-like detail on each of the shelves, so we picked up a yard of lace fabric for an impromptu stencil and got our spray paint on.

1 Use medium-grit sandpaper or a sanding block to lightly remove any glossy finish. Then apply a coat of primer and, once that's dry, a coat of your base color to each shelf (ours was a satin-finish white).

2 Once the base coat is dry, cut your lace to fit and lay it flat on the furniture's surface. Any raised areas might mess up your pattern, so you really want to trim it so it lies nice and flat.

3 Lightly mist the surface with spray paint (we used Valspar's Everglade Glen), almost allowing the spray to rain down on the lace and avoiding a direct shot as much as possible. Don't worry about getting good coverage on the rest of the piece of furniture yet; just focus on the area where you want to have the lace pattern (the top, or the shelves).

4 Immediately (and carefully) remove the lace and allow everything to dry thoroughly.

(continued)

5 Once the sprayed surface is completely dry, protect your pattern (we used a scrap piece of cardboard that was taped with painter's tape around the edges) and then spray the rest of the piece. This may require two coats to get good coverage.

6 Once the paint has dried, remove the painter's tape and admire your handiwork. The stenciled part will most likely be soft and imperfect, so just embrace the extra charm.

Make It **Accessible**

Susan and Andrew knew the day might soon come when one of their aging parents would move in. Keeping someone with mobility challenges in mind may seem daunting, but they used it to inspire some smart choices during their renovation, such as a stylish seamless shower entry and some sleek grab bars.

Susan admits that finding attractive grab bars was a challenge, but Google eventually led her to some modern options by Invisia.

survey says: 17% of the people we polled have a freestanding tub in their master bathroom. 100% of the authors of this book are envious.

Wall Covering
for the Win

Most bathrooms are modestly sized, so they're a great place for special details.

1 WAINSCOTING. Adding beadboard or other decorative moldings to your bathroom not only amps up the architecture in boring spaces (we're looking at you, half bathrooms) but also can be a quick fix. Jenny and Jay loathed their bathroom's maroon and teal tile, so they covered it up with twenty-five-dollar beadboard panels. Adding a trim piece around the top finished things off, and it was a 100 percent demo-free way to update their room on a budget.

2 WALLPAPER. Small spaces are a perfect excuse to take wallpaper for a spin, whether you go with a classic pattern or something more whimsical, like this collage-inspired design that Sarah and Peter used to wake up a basic half bath. Small rooms won't require as many rolls, and you can cut costs even more by just wallpapering above a half wall of tile or wainscoting.

Boosting the Happy Factor

Sarah and Peter
live with
Viggo (age 8), Beppe (age 5), and Maja (the cat)
and describe their home as
Homey, Messy, and Always Changing

Sarah and Peter live in Sweden with their two sons, and not only do they face the challenge of living in just 900 square feet but they also do it in a country that sees limited sunlight for many months of the year! As their bathroom (opposite, right) shows, they don't use lack of either space or light as an excuse to play it safe, opting for lots of pattern to make the most of small rooms and using color to keep things cheery and bright.

1

2

Doodle in the Bathroom

This cheeky update is for those who love the look of wallpaper but worry that the humidity of a bathroom will be its downfall . . . literally. Instead you can try your hand at making a graphic pattern with an oil paint pen. Sharpie makes some great colors. (We used one in "metallic silver.") First we painted our hall bathroom a dark color (Starless Night by Behr), and once the paint was dry, we went to town drawing playful flowers of all sorts. The result was an easy high-impact look that we enjoyed until we could tackle a more thorough overhaul, which you can see on page 176.

Practice your drawings with pen on paper first, and if you hate them once they're on the wall, one coat of primer will cover them right up.

I doodle in the backyard.

survey says: **66% of the people we polled say their master bathroom needs renovating.**

Play with **Materials**

Being creative in a bathroom isn't just about what you put on the walls—it can also be about what you make the walls out of. Take cues from some of these creative bathrooms.

1 RECLAIMED MATERIALS. Eric's construction job often lands him some cool leftovers. This blue-green wainscoting was originally an old porch ceiling, the ceiling planks were formerly oak flooring, and Eric made the brick floor by shaving old bricks on a masonry saw to create thinner brick "tiles."

2 TILE WAINSCOT. Monica and Dean always pictured this tile on the floor of their half bath, but the builder continued the wood floor into the space. Their solution? Use the tile on the wall instead!

3 WALL-TO-WALL WOOD. Joey and Jeff gave their master bathroom a rustic sauna vibe by planking the walls (and ceiling!) with pine boards. It gives the space a warm, cozy feel that tile doesn't always achieve.

survey says: 42% of the people we polled don't have an en suite master bathroom.

3

Customize a **Vanity**

Prepackaged vanities and sinks are often affordable and easy solutions. But with a little extra effort, you can assemble one of your own that looks less off-the-shelf and more true-to-you. All it takes is four key ingredients.

1 A BASE. Have fun picking out an interesting base. Wendy chose an old dresser with chipped paint for hers (opposite), because of its charm and generous storage. Susan had a sawhorse-inspired piece (below) built out of reclaimed wood by a local carpenter. Whatever you choose, just make sure it can be adapted to accommodate plumbing.

2 A COUNTER. Stone yards often sell remnant pieces at a discount, so this is a great route to take for smaller bathrooms. Most stores will even cut them for you. Susan actually found her piece of black granite at a Habitat for Humanity ReStore and then had the base built to fit it.

3 A SINK. Vessel sinks like the ones shown here (which sit on top of the counter) are the easiest types of sink to add yourself. Integrated or undermount options can also be incorporated, but you may need the help of a stone yard or a carpenter to sink them into your counter and vanity.

4 A FAUCET. Make sure you plan for faucet placement, especially if it means getting holes cut in the counter. Wendy and Susan avoided this (and maximized sink size) by choosing wall-mounted and sink-mounted versions, respectively.

Step Up a Stool

If you've got wee ones around, chances are there is a stool somewhere nearby, or in your near future. If the cheap plastic varieties aren't your thing, hit up your favorite craft or discount furniture store for a wooden one that you can put your own spin on. (We found this one at HomeGoods.) We stenciled on a pattern, but you could also add stripes with painter's tape, personalize it with a painted initial, or give it a dipped effect by painting only the bottom half.

1 If the stool is unfinished or not your desired base color, use a **stain-blocking primer** to prime it and paint it with **latex paint in a satin finish.**

2 We cut down our **stencil**, which was from Royal Design Studio, so it was only slightly larger than the step, just to make it easier to work with.

3 Use **painter's tape** to hold the stencil in place.

4 Apply a light coat of paint (we used Benjamin Moore's Cinco de Mayo in a satin finish) over the stencil with a **small foam roller,** being careful not to glob it on, or if you'd prefer, lightly dab the paint on with a foam pouncer.

5 Remove the stencil and repeat the process on the other step. We used two different parts of one larger stencil, just for fun.

Make the Most of a **Small Bathroom**

Katja and Frank converted a first-floor powder room into a full bathroom to better serve guests. Here are some tricks they used to make the room seem more spacious.

✳ **MAXIMIZED LIGHT.** Hanging a pendant in front of the mirror, rather than mounting one on the wall above, allows more light to bounce around the room.

✳ **GLASS SHOWER.** The room needed a shower, but to make it visually disappear as much as possible, they installed a glass enclosure that doesn't block the window.

✳ **FLOATING VANITY.** Mounting the vanity on the wall makes the room feel less heavy and allows for more floor space.

✳ **WALL-MOUNTED FAUCET.** To keep the vanity depth down, they had the faucet installed on the wall so they could still use a generously sized sink.

✳ **BONUS STORAGE.** They found room for a narrow cabinet (less than 6 inches deep!) between the toilet and the window, creating a hidden storage spot for extra toilet paper rolls.

✳ **THE RIGHT TOILET.** They chose a "compact elongated" model that combines the smaller size of a round-front toilet with the comfort of a larger elongated version, saving at least 3 inches of space.

That bathroom looks like a mansion to me.

survey says: "Over!" is how 77% of the people we polled say they prefer their toilet paper to be hung.

Contain Yourself

To store your small bathroom items—from toothbrushes and cotton swabs to even small plants—think beyond the standard cup or glass jar. Thrift shops, yard sales, and antiques stores are overflowing with unique, charming, and budget-friendly finds. I mean, c'mon, who doesn't love a cheeky three-dollar wooden clog–turned–succulent pot?

Get **Peggy** with It

Pegboards are great organizers for just about any space. You can pick up a panel for less than ten dollars at a home-improvement store, and there are an increasing variety of hooks, baskets, and other add-ons to use with them. Turn the page to learn how to make a custom shape and bring even more personality to the organizing party.

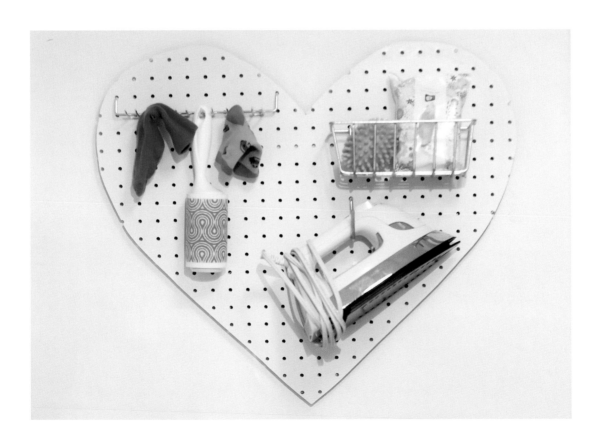

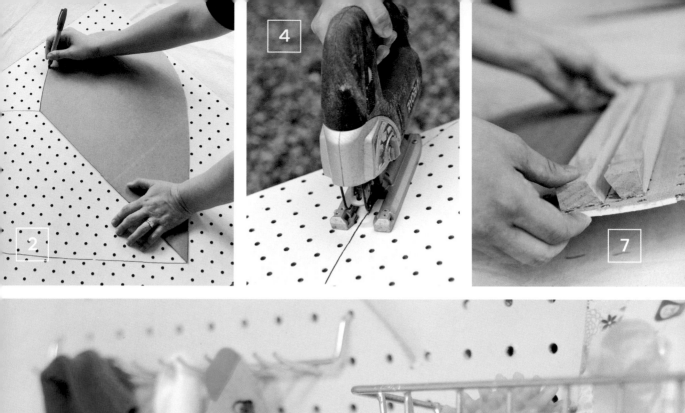

1 Sketch your desired shape on **cardboard** and cut it out to make your template. If you're cutting a symmetrical shape, you can draw and cut just half.

2 Using your cardboard template, trace your shape onto the **pegboard**. For a symmetrical shape, trace your half template and then flip it over to draw an exact mirror image on the other side.

3 Secure your pegboard over the edge of a work surface with **clamps**, or ask a helper to hold it in place with you, being sure to keep your hands away from the area to be cut.

4 Use a **jigsaw** to carefully cut along your traced line, pausing to reposition the pegboard as needed so the area to be cut overhangs your work surface slightly.

5 Once the board is cut, lightly sand the edges to smooth any roughness. Paint the pegboard if you'd like to add color.

6 Pegboards must float off the wall slightly so there's room for the hooks to go through. A simple option is to glue **1-by-2-inch blocks** to the back corners of the pegboard so it doesn't rest against the wall. Then you can screw directly through those blocks into the wall, being sure to hit a stud or an anchor.

7 Another option is to create a cleat, like the one shown. For this we sliced our 1-by-2-inch board on a table saw at a slight angle. The top portion of the cleat is glued to the pegboard, while the bottom is screwed into the wall. This helps the pegboard securely float off the wall, without having visible screws on the front.

8 Once the pegboard is hung, attach hooks and baskets to your liking. This might even be the spot where single socks can hang out until they're joyfully reunited with their mates.

Add Life to Your
Laundry Zone

Katherine and Richard were blessed with a generously sized basement laundry room. The only catch? A large portion of the space was going unused. So they added some fun for their whole family by squeezing in an awesome little art space.

Double-Duty Table

A large sawhorse table anchors the room, giving the kids a great surface for drawing. At night when the kids are in bed, the paper can roll back up so Mom and Dad have room to fold clothes.

Smile-Inducing Shelves

Thanks to the washer and dryer's pedestal bases, which conceal laundry supplies, the room's built-ins are freed up to be happily stocked with craft stuff.

survey says: The three most common locations for a washer and dryer among the people we surveyed are: in a laundry room (32%), in the basement (23%), and in a laundry closet or nook (18%).

Wake Up a **Boring Laundry Room**

WEEKEND PROJECT

A boxy and bland laundry room is a great place to try wallpaper, but it can still be scary to jump on the bandwagon. Is it hard to install? What if you hate it in a few years? Well, we took it for a spin in a family member's laundry room and learned that it's not that scary. And look at the difference it made in this windowless space for just sixty dollars!

Your wallpaper should come with hanging instructions that are specific to that maker (this was from Spoonflower), so here are some general tips that we learned along the way.

✳ **TRY A SELF-ADHESIVE WALLPAPER WITH GLUE BUILT IN.** It's still not a mess-free process (you need to wet the wallpaper to activate the glue), but you won't have to deal with applying a separate adhesive.

✳ **CONSIDER REMOVABLE VARIETIES.** Commitment-phobes will appreciate that many of these self-adhering papers are easily removable and leftover glue wipes off with warm water (as is the case with the paper we used).

Before

(continued)

* **PREPARE FOR SPLASHES AND DRIPS.** Submerging a 2-foot-wide roll in water takes more than your average bucket. We used a bathtub and relied on the bucket to transport the soaked roll back to our work space. Definitely keep towels handy, especially when you start pressing the paper onto the wall.

* **GIVE YOURSELF LOTS OF ROOM.** Working with a 12-foot-long roll requires lots of floor space when it comes time to "bookend" the wet roll to activate the glue. We laid out two fabric drop cloths in a nearby room for this step, which involves folding the two ends back toward the middle of the wallpaper strip.

* **HAVE A HELPER.** This wallpaper can be fairly forgiving (it allowed for a certain amount of peeling, repositioning, and smoothing to get any bubbles or wrinkles out), but it was still invaluable to have two sets of hands and eyes working together to hang it.

* **BUY A SMOOTHER.** A plastic wallpaper smoother costs just a couple of bucks, but it's great for giving your paper one last pass after you've gotten it mostly applied with a damp sponge.

Make It **Multi-Use**

Laundry rooms can do more than just clean
your clothes. Amy and Graham also use theirs to
house pet bowls and extra dog food, so they're not
tripping over them in heavier-traffic rooms like
the kitchen.

Amy added some
pet-themed art as
a fun nod to the
room's extra use.

ENTRY SPACES

Sherry says

WHETHER YOU'VE GOT A FORMAL FOYER, a laundry-slash-mudroom, or just a living room that randomly sports a front door, the rooms we enter into every day not only need to provide a warm welcome home, but often need to be super functional too. Unless you're one of those miracle people who can live without shoes, car keys, or bags.

Both of our first two homes lacked a proper entryway. The front door of each one swung unceremoniously into a living or dining room, so when guests came over, it was like, "Hello! . . . and watch out for the couch." We tried defining the entry zone with large consoles that sort of doubled as entry tables, but mostly we were just grateful that those front doors went largely unused.

We entered daily through the side or back doors, since they were closer to where we parked. That's also where we directed friends and family to spare them the obligatory walk down the front path. In both houses, those "real" entry doors opened into our laundry spaces. So while it wasn't much prettier for our guests, it was at least a more functional place to kick off shoes or hang up a coat.

When we purchased our current home, it felt like a gift from above to finally have a proper foyer: a room whose primary function is to look pretty when you open the front door. (Not to mention that it has not one but two coat closets, one of which we use for toy storage.) It's actually one of the first rooms we redid after moving in, by stripping the floral

Our second home's front door opened right into the dining room.

wallpaper, painting the dated blue trim, hanging a new light fixture, and adding a cheerful color to both sides of the front door. We wanted to celebrate not only the concept of finally having a foyer but also that it is a great "happiness investment" to turn a centrally located room that we pass through several times a day into a space we enjoy.

But in all of our excitement over finally having a foyer, we sort of overlooked the fact that we were missing that other type of entryway. You know, that super-functional space where shoes can pile up and bags can be dropped. Yup, now the door that we use most regularly—the one leading from the garage—dumps us right into the kitchen. And with the fridge on one side of it and the stove on the other, there's not exactly a convenient spot to hang your coat. Sad trombone.

A spare closet in our entryway provides some great toy storage.

If there's one thing we've learned, it's that every house has its challenge (or ten). For now we've created a makeshift drop zone a few steps beyond the kitchen door by tucking a basket beneath a built-in desk to wrangle shoes. And a closet around the corner houses coats, while mail and keys just land on the kitchen counter. It's not perfect, but it works well enough until our big remodel, when we hope to reconfigure the appliances and sneak in a mini mudroom that looks built into the rest of the kitchen. Someday . . .

One **Drop Zone,** Three Ways

Sure, a table or chest of drawers in your entryway is a great place to toss keys and mail, but the space above it can serve a number of functions too. Here are three ideas.

1 SHELVES. Whether you're using them to extend your drop zone space or just for decorative purposes, simple shelves are easy to add—or even make yourself. These are just stained planks of wood that we rested on two stock metal brackets from the home-improvement store that we spray painted oil-rubbed bronze.

2 MIRROR. Good for more than giving you a chance to check your outfit for cat hair on the way out the door, mirrors also help bounce light around and make any small area feel more spacious.

3 ART OR PHOTOS. While any collection of large- or smaller-scale artwork is a great way to showcase your home's personality, it can be especially nice to frame favorite family photos to send you on your way and to greet you when you return.

Shop the office-supply aisle for some bonus storage, like this woven file system for incoming mail, outgoing library books, and a dog leash or two.

survey says: It's a tie! 50% of the people we polled use their front door most often, while the other 50% use their back, side, or garage doors instead.

Hang or lean a clock to see just how late you're running.

1

2

3

Upgrading Our
Garage Entry

Although the door that leads from our garage to the kitchen doesn't pack the same curb-appeal punch that a front door does, it's the entrance *we* use every day, so we wanted it to be a little more welcoming (and a lot more functional). Here's how we made that back wall work a lot harder, and look a lot more cheerful, for under a hundred dollars.

Before

✳ **A DRAMATIC DOOR.** We love the happy teal color (Blue Lake by Benjamin Moore) that we chose for our front door, so we also wanted it to greet us when we enter through the garage. We primed the door first, and then painted it with a small foam roller in a semigloss finish, making our formerly dingy door a lot more fun.

✳ **FRESH WALLS.** We gave the walls a crisp coat of white paint, which helped disguise the fuse box and the cinder blocks (we primed those first). We also added a storage bench for extra function and a place to set things down when we approach the door.

✳ **SUBSTANTIAL STAIRS.** We added risers by nailing 1-by-10-inch boards under each stair tread and applied a fresh coat of porch and floor paint, giving the steps a more finished look.

(continued)

✳ A RUBBER RUNNER.
The old carpeting on
the stairs was worn and
fraying, so we pulled it up
and swapped in a rubber
doormat that we cut into
three equal sections with
scissors. The rubber
stays in place nicely, so
they don't slide around
underfoot, but they still lift
right off for easy cleaning.

✳ SIMPLE TRIM. In
addition to installing
molding around the door
to polish it off, we nailed a
strip of 1-by-3-inch wood
across the surrounding
wall to break up that big
blank expanse and add
some visual interest. It
also creates a natural spot
for storage hooks without
being bound to stud
placement.

Our garage is home to plenty of
less-than-attractive things, so
we chose to hang the brightest
items on this wall for the liveliest
view when we pull in.

Fake an **Entryway**

Many homes lack a designated entry room (like our missing mudroom). Luckily, you can fake one with a few simple additions. Courtney and Jack carved out this entry zone where their front door opens into the living room. They purchased items in the same finishes as the living room furniture so they feel less out of place. Here are three helpful elements to consider adding to your own entryway.

1 A PLACE TO HANG STUFF. A traditional coatrack or even just a few hooks added to the wall will do the job of keeping jackets, backpacks, and purses off the floor and within easy reach.

2 A SURFACE TO DROP STUFF. Add a shallow console table, a small side table, or even a floating shelf for a quick spot to toss keys or mail.

3 A SYSTEM FOR WRANGLING SHOES. It could be as simple as kicking them off under a console table, or you could try stashing them in a basket or on a low-profile shoe rack.

100% of Chihuahuas were excluded from this poll.

survey says: 33% of the people we polled have an entry door that opens into their living room.

TIP

Look for double-duty pieces. This mirror came with built-in hooks, but you can DIY one by adding the hardware yourself.

Sneak a **Mudroom** into Your Kitchen

Katherine and Richard's back door opens right into their kitchen, so during their remodel they got creative and integrated some serious mudroom functions right into the cabinets they added next to their back door. This floor-to-ceiling mudroom cubby blends seamlessly with the rest of the room thanks to doors that mimic their kitchen cabinetry. The lower ones corral their kids' stuff, and they use the higher ones for their own items, like coats, laptops, and purses.

Add a charging station.
Creating a space in your entryway to charge your devices—even if it means adding an outlet to a concealed cubby or cabinet—can help ensure that your phone is juiced up and easy to find.

survey says: 17% of the people we polled have an entry door that opens into their kitchen.

Make Your **Foyer** Feel Grand

We're not all as blessed in the entryway department as Jenny and Jay are with their formal foyer, but at least we can steal inspiration for whatever sized room we may step into.

✳ **LUXE LIGHTING.** If you're short on floor space, use the ceiling as a spot to add interest or a little sparkle. Even if your ceilings are low, you can find flush-mount lights that mimic crystal chandeliers at big-box stores these days.

✳ **BIG ARTWORK.** Finding a large painting or framing an oversized print will create a great focal point and lend some sophistication that dinkier frames or wall hangings might not be able to replicate.

✳ **FINE FABRICS.** Whether on window treatments, an upholstered chair, or even a simple bench, finding a spot for some pretty fabric can lend softness and elegance to your entry space.

✳ **ARCHITECTURAL INTEREST.** A surefire way to give any room a sense of importance is to add interesting details. Maybe a pair of columns won't fit in yours, but consider adding some wainscoting, wood-planked walls, or even some beams on the ceiling overhead.

✳ **GREENERY.** There's no denying that plants add freshness and life to any room. And fear not if you have a black thumb—we've found some pretty great faux varieties that have even fooled our green-thumbed friends (faux succulents are especially convincing).

Get **Crate**-ative

If you don't have one of those magazine-worthy mudrooms (or the space or budget to add one), sometimes you can tack on some smaller-scale function in a more budget-friendly way. These colorful crates are inexpensive and great for kids. (They can each have a crate or two to use as their own cubby.)

1 Purchase enough **wooden storage crates** (ours are from Jo-Ann Fabric and Crafts) to suit your space and your needs and decide on the arrangement. We chose an orderly stacked grouping with enough room between the crates to put things on or below them. You can arrange the crates asymmetrically or in a random layout if you'd like.

2 Place the crates on a **drop cloth**, making sure you have created a protected area if you're using spray paint.

3 Prime and paint your crates with a **roller** and a **brush** or **spray paint with a built-in primer.** (We chose Rust-Oleum's Lagoon, Seaside, and Fossil.) Expect to apply at least two coats to ensure good coverage in all the nooks and crannies.

4 Once the crates are dry and ready to hang, use a **pencil** and a **level** to mark your holes. You can choose to drill directly through the crates (a pilot hole is recommended to prevent splitting) or just rest the crate's top slat on the screws. If your screw doesn't go into a stud, use **heavy-duty anchors** for added support.

Have a **Designated Spot** for Everything

We've all heard the saying "A place for everything, and everything in its place," and the entryway is the perfect spot to put this idea into practice. It doesn't mean every place needs to be pretty and expertly organized at all times (John's keys and wallet just get tossed into a bowl), but knowing where those things are when you're rushing out the door can cut stress and save time.

1 DOUBLE YOUR DROP ZONE. Try nesting two pieces for twice the surface space. Elisabeth tucked this hand-me-down trunk under a Parsons table to create a two-tiered area for laying out things like her purse, a stack of mail, and her laptop. A trunk or a storage ottoman can also add hidden stash space and a place to sit and remove your shoes.

2 SUIT YOUR NEEDS. Carrie and Matt typically enter and exit through their garage, and use the front door only to take their dogs for a walk. So they decided that area's best use is to wrangle leashes, balls, and other pet items in a charming wooden cubby organizer.

survey says: Two-thirds of the people we polled prefer concealed storage for hiding stuff in their entryway over open storage for easy access.

Dresser Up Your Entry Organization

Although they're usually found in bedrooms, dressers can be a hardworking option for your entryway too. Thanks to these six generously sized drawers, Emily and Todd have tons of concealed storage for their family of five. This yard-sale dresser houses everything from umbrellas, gloves, and extra keys to sunglasses, lint brushes, bug spray, and leashes.

survey says: The five items that the people we polled struggled most to keep organized in their entryway were:
1. Shoes (71%)   2. Mail (46%)   3. Bags and backpacks (41%)   4. Coats (29%)   5. Pet stuff (13%)

Wall hooks keep school bags off the ground.

The metal door doubles as a magnet board.

A galvanized bucket corrals shoes.

Five **Entryway** Additions

If you feel like your entry is falling flat or you're stuck on what to do next, here are a handful of ideas to get you going again.

1 INVEST IN A SHOWSTOPPING DOOR. This one isn't a bold color, but the linear panes and deep ebony tone create a graphic and modern element you can soak up from inside and out.

2 ADD CONCEALED STORAGE. When looking for an entry table or drop zone piece, try to find something with drawers or even a shallow cabinet for bonus space that doesn't have to be kept as tidy. We got this narrow beauty for a steal at HomeGoods.

3 PROTECT THE FLOOR PRETTILY. Choosing a rug in a rich tone with a fair amount of pattern can save you from fretting over obvious dust and dirt that a lighter rug might show off a lot more.

4 HANG SOMETHING UNEXPECTED. Choosing something quirky, like a hanging bud vase or an old iron mailbox, adds interest. Plus, the mailbox equals extra storage space for things like spare keys, sunglasses, or mail.

5 DON'T OVERTHINK IT. A long dish can be an easy drop-zone spot for incoming or outgoing mail, and a decorative plate (Anthropologie has some pretty ones) is the perfect casual spot for keys.

Look **Up**

With entry halls and mudroom walls often serving super-functional purposes, consider looking to your ceiling as a place to play around. We painted our foyer ceiling one shade darker than the sand-colored walls (and one finish glossier) for a little something extra. Joey and Jeff went even bolder: Utilizing their high ceilings and some inexpensive scrap wood strips from a mill shop, they created a textured archway in their entry that feels unique and full of character.

Something Different

Joey and Jeff
live with
Eleanor (age 3), Sophy John (age 2), and Felipe (the dog)
and describe their home as
Modern, Rustic, and Efficient

Jeff got the construction bug after years of volunteering for Habitat for Humanity, and he now owns his own custom-building company specializing in unique modern homes. But for their own house, he and Joey wanted a cozier feel, so instead of drywall, they used wood on the walls and ceilings to give every room a warm, rustic feeling. And features like this slatted ceiling also remind Jeff of his days growing up on boats! See more of their home on pages 41, 87, 169, and 193.

survey says: The five most popular door colors of the people we polled were:
1. Brown or tan (22%)   2. White (21%)   3. Black (15%)   4. Red (13%)   5. Blue (11%)

Stretch Yourself

Small spaces are a great spot to experiment with something bold—like this punchy wallpaper that Susan and Andrew used in their formerly nondescript foyer. They wanted white walls throughout most of their home (both to highlight their art and to combat poor natural light), but in their foyer they used a few rolls of wallpaper to create a super-cheery entry hall to welcome them home every day.

Sneak In Something
Meaningful

Your entryway walls are a great opportunity to hang something that makes you smile every time you walk by. Amy and Graham adorned their classic foyer (opposite) with a grid of old black-and-white family photos. They're a great fit for their traditional style and bring a heavy dose of family history—some date to the 1800s!

No photos? No problem.
You can add a meaningful touch to your walls with other artwork, like these state-specific tea towels that Carrie and Matt scored for four dollars apiece. Each one represents a place they've lived or visit often, so they stretched them over canvases to line the hall near their entryway.

Add Some
Entryway Shine

Nothing takes a piece of furniture from basic
to Beyoncé like adding a glossy metallic finish.
But you don't want anything that looks cheap
or plastic-y, so we tested a slew of options to pin
down our favorite metallic paint that has the most
high-end metal-like shine. Here's what worked.

1 Place your furniture on
a **drop cloth** in a safe-to-
spray area outside.

2 Remove any drawers
so you can work on them
separately and unscrew
any hardware that you
don't want painted.

3 For previously painted
or stained items, rough
up the surface with
sandpaper to remove any
glossy finish.

4 Wipe down the entire
piece with a **damp rag**
to remove dirt or sanding
dust.

5 **Primer** helps with
paint adhesion. We used
Rust-Oleum Clean Metal
Primer.

6 After testing paint
that can be brushed or
rolled, and various spray
paints, our favorite was
Rust-Oleum Bright Coat
Metallic Finish spray
paint in Chrome for its
believable metal-like
shine. Just look at those
legs on the page to the left
(speaking of Beyoncé, *to
the left, to the left*).

7 Shaking your spray
paint can is critical to
getting an even, mirrorlike
finish with this type of
paint. Shake vigorously
before you begin and pause
frequently to reshake the
can as you apply thin and
even coats according to
the directions. Beware
of coating too heavily,
especially on vertical
surfaces that may drip.

(continued)

8 Allow the piece to dry completely and recoat, especially if there are areas that are less shiny than you'd like. (We went through two cans to finish this table—but, boy, does she gleam!)

9 Reassemble drawers, reattach hardware, and resist the urge to shout "Bling, bling!" (whispering it is totally okay).

Get **Your Gear** off the Floor

Keeping your floors clear is one of the best tricks for making a space feel cleaner and less like a literal dumping ground. Here are two tricks to encourage that phenomenon.

1 **FLOAT YOUR FURNITURE.** This storage bench not only helps keep shoes off the ground, but mounted to the wall, it also makes the room feel bigger by adding more visible floor space.

2 **WORK YOUR WALLS TWICE AS HARD.** By adding two rows of hooks, one for grown-ups and a lower one for their young girls, Joey and Jeff double their chances that things will get hung up. They even mounted a small wire basket to wrangle smaller items like gloves and scarves.

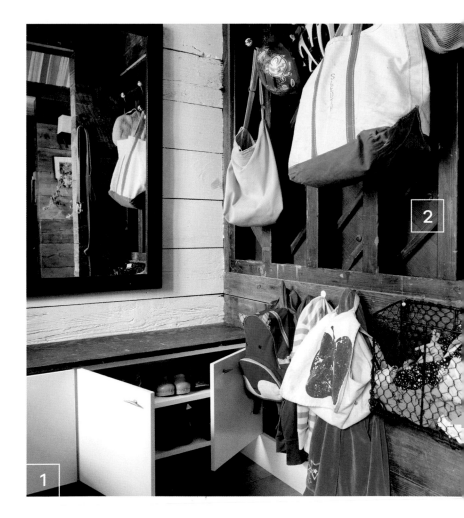

Paint On a Pattern

If wallpaper is too expensive or feels like too much of a commitment, paint is a cheap and easy alternative. You can achieve a wallpaper effect with a stencil, like the oversized medallion that Jenny and Jay used across from their front door (opposite). Or simple 12-inch stripes, like these by Joey and Jeff's stairway (below), can add tons of interest for just the cost of paint and some painter's tape.

TIP

*Luxe up
your paint job.*
Consider adding an
accent with extra-glossy—
or even metallic—paint,
which can give your
painted pattern a
posh touch.

Be Brave with **Flooring**

Walls shouldn't have all the fun, right?

Add Pattern

We've stenciled patterns on our fair share of floors, but Sunny took things one step further in her house with a homemade stencil and two tones of wood stain instead of paint. She used contact paper to mask off the pattern on her freshly sanded floor, and then applied a very light coat of the darker stain using a rag. Once the stain was dry, she removed the stencil and went over the entire floor with the lighter color, then finished things off with a glossy sealer.

Mix Up Materials

While tile is always a great durable choice for heavy-traffic entryways, Nicole and Jason wanted something with extra character, so they chose worn bricks for their mudroom. They knew it would easily stand up to their dog Henri's frequent use (he passes in and out all day), and the bricks were reclaimed from old Chicago buildings, so they add so much character—some even have old paint on them!

Make the Right
First Impression

Entryways are usually a visitor's first glimpse of your home, so ask yourself if yours is saying the right things.

✳ DOES IT SET THE STAGE FOR THE REST OF YOUR HOME? If your entry's decor isn't as exciting as the rooms beyond it, consider adding colors, patterns, or finishes that are found elsewhere in your house.

✳ DOES IT HINT AT WHO LIVES THERE? You don't have to literally hang family portraits (although personal photos are always sweet), but it's nice when an entryway tells visitors a little something about the people who live there (like that they love bold art, rustic textures, or travel, for example).

Mad for Mod

Aletha and Greg
live with
Eames (age 3) and Olive (the dog)
and describe their home as
Casual, Curated, and Calm

Aletha and Greg are passionate about all things midcentury modern, and they fell hard for this Orla Kiely wallpaper that hangs in their dining space (left), which is near their entryway. They loved it so much that it inspired a custom railing that Greg made himself (opposite). It was his first adventure in welding! Taking something that's usually so standard—like a railing—and making it special is a great way to put your stamp on your home, and to give guests a taste of your style as soon as they step through the door.

Add Some
Unexpected Interest

Crown molding, wainscoting, and patterned walls are great ways to amp up basic or cookie-cutter spaces, but you can also accent a few other run-of-the-mill features, like Meg did in her entryway.

* She used an old salvaged door whose chipped paint and vintage glass doorknob added instant charm to this formerly basic bedroom entrance.

* She painted the stair railing soft green for an unexpected wink of color on an otherwise standard staircase.

* She used decorative paper on this door's glass panel to provide privacy for her roommate. It can also turn any glass display case into concealed storage.

WORKING SPACES

Sherry says

JOHN AND I MET (and covertly fell in love) while working at a midtown advertising agency in New York City back in 2005, but for as long as we have lived together, I've worked from home. (After trading the urban jungle for the greener pastures of Richmond, Virginia, I was grateful to be able to tackle client copywriting from home as a freelancer.) So trying to carve out some sort of dedicated "home office" area has been a constant in our homeownership adventures from day one. I say home office in quotes because it took a few years for my "work spaces" (there go those quotes again) to take the form of a truer office—as in, something with walls, a desk, and even a chair.

We moved to our first apartment together from New York City in a minivan and had barely any furniture. We bought a bed on our drive down to our new place in Richmond, but other than that, our apartment was stocked mostly with old family hand-me-downs. We actually got a desk from John's sister, but it quickly became the kitchen/dining table since we didn't have one of those.

So my first office consisted of me sitting on the floor cross-legged with my laptop resting on the corner of the media cabinet that also housed our TV. Awesome, no?

By the time we moved into our first house, I had upgraded to a proper desk space with a chair (so novel!) and my back was eternally grateful. My best friend had given us a Parsons table as a wedding gift, and it still has a place in our office. (Half of this book was written there!) Back when we got it, we just slipped it into the corner of our living room, so I still

My pitiful desk-less and chair-less "home office" in our first apartment.

didn't have a home office per se. And let's be real, whatever copywriting I was working on after hours was usually done on my laptop in front of the TV.

It wasn't until John started to work from home full-time in 2010 that we decided we needed to create a legitimate office for ourselves—even if it meant cramming a skinny double desk that we made from an old hollow-core door into our guest room. It wasn't the most spacious work area you've ever seen, but it did the job as we did ours.

Ever since, there has been something motivating and rewarding about creating work spaces in our homes. We typically flounder around for a while without one (finding a spot on the sofa or at the kitchen table to sit with a laptop) and then when we finally commit to creating a dedicated office space, we're both like "Um . . . why did we wait so long?" Yes sir, the pull of the couch or the kitchen table can be strong, but it turns out we can focus a lot better when we're working in an area that's built for the job.

Adding an art desk for the kids to our home office helps the whole family "work" together.

Squeeze in a
Work Space

Even if you don't work from home, more and more people are finding the need to carve out a productivity-based space there. In fact, more than 80 percent of our survey respondents reported having a designated room or spot in their home for work tasks, although most of them aren't using it for their full-time job.

Home offices have only recently gained in popularity in most residential construction, so many of us with older homes are left with the need to find a spot to devote to an at-home work area. This often means stealing space in a spare bedroom, using a corner of a kitchen or living room, or creating an entirely new zone somewhere else.

I take naps like it's my job. Oh, wait, it is.

survey says: 37% of the people we polled use a spare bedroom as a home office.

Emily and Todd added a double-desk area behind a knee wall in their basement with two simple rectangular tables placed in an L shape. This layout creates two good-sized work spaces instead of just one, which comes in handy with two teens and a five-year-old under one roof.

Wrangle Your **Wires**

Cords are a necessary evil in this electronic age, but that doesn't make them any prettier to look at. We've found that the best solutions for taming the twisted mess are often the simplest. Here are three easy fixes that anyone can try.

1 BRING IN A WIRE HIDER. Simply adding an object under an open desk, like the garden stool that Richard used in his sunroom office, may be all you need to stop cords from being as obvious. Nothing beats how easy it is, except for maybe how easy it still is to access your power strip.

(continued)

survey says: 65% of the people we polled use a laptop as their primary computer.

2 **HANG A BASKET.** Any time we've attempted some complex system of clips and zip ties to get our cords off the floor, it all fell apart the first time we had to add or remove a wire from the mix. But with this solution—a cheap wire basket hung right under the desk with removable 3M hooks—it's easy to lift the basket off when you need to make a plug switch. No careful cord sorting or rewrapping required.

3 PRETTY 'EM UP. Even the best cord wrangler can't control those cords that snake up above our desks. But you can dress them up a bit with electrical tape. We found a three-dollar roll in a happy yellow color and used short strips to cheer up this exposed lamp cord.

A Living Room Turned Art Studio

Sunny and Read
live with
Presley (age 17); Whit (age 16); Beck (age 12); Blackjack, Lila, Mabel (three Labs); and some chickens in a coop out back
and describe their home as
Livable, Creative, and Constantly Changing

As Sunny's painting hobby grew into a profession, operating out of an off-site studio made her feel too disconnected from the activities at home. So her family decided to convert the front living room into a space where Sunny could paint and still be available to her three children.

Creative Clipping
Sunny found that digging around for the right paint colors in a drawer was often frustratingly inefficient, so she began pinning them up using binder clips—a cheap and easy solution for keeping all of her colors in view.

survey says: We asked people to describe the nature of their home-based business. Here's a sampling of the wide-ranging responses: calligrapher, wedding videographer, piano teacher, home-day-care provider, cake decorator, financial planner, stationery designer, and bean farmer.

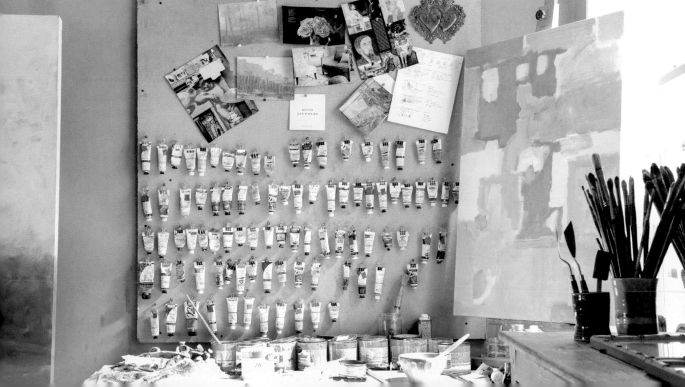

Carve Out a
Craft Space

Most sewing and crafting around here used to come with a time limit, since whatever work surface it required (usually the kitchen counter or table) needed to be cleared for a meal within a few hours. Plus lugging the sewing machine in and out of the closet didn't exactly encourage more projects (things got put off for days, and then weeks. . .), so it was definitely worth it to turn an unused wall in our guest room into a full-time crafting and sewing desk. Here's what we added.

✳ **STORAGE.** We scored one of these drawered bases in Ikea's discounted as-is section and later found a matching one on Craigslist for a steal. Now they provide some great storage for items like craft paints, brushes, paint pens, thread spools, and decorative paper.

✳ **A WORK SURFACE.** After cutting a store-bought 2-by-6-foot wood panel down to 60 inches, we beefed it up with a tiered detail, courtesy of another panel that we cut a half inch shorter on each side and nailed to the underside of the first board. Then we primed it, and painted it semigloss white.

Ditch the **Boring Built-Ins**

Nicole and Jason knew that the subtle gray walls in their office could handle a big dose of their favorite color, although it did take some test swatches to get it just right. (They landed on Amazon Moss by Benjamin Moore.) The vibrant hue feels happy and never boring—and it breathes a ton of life into the room where Jason works full-time.

survey says: A large desk is the top answer from the people we polled on the ultimate luxury in a home office.

With such a showstopping color on the built-ins, they didn't want anything too visually demanding or heavy for a much-needed floating desk. Enter this acrylic number that gives them a great bonus work (and coloring) surface.

A Graphic Designer's Graphic Home Office

Carrie and Matt
live with
Marco and Atticus (the dogs) and Sprocket (the cat)
and describe their home as
Happy, Geeky, and Cozy

Carrie's spare-bedroom-turned-office is full of energetic decor and inspiration (something she needs daily for her design work). But working full-time, and trying to keep her work from spilling over into other areas of the house, also means she has to pack the room with a whole lot of function.

Rolling Printing Station

Carrie does a lot of oversized printing, so she always has her printer at the ready. The drawers below it store paper, and they sit on casters so she can easily roll them out and feed the large sheets through the back. Creating a zone with everything you need for a specific task can save you from running to all corners of a room.

Shipping Closet

In addition to her client work, Carrie also sells printed items through an online shop, so her husband, Matt, helped her turn the office's closet into a mini shipping and supply center. Shelves store flat items like prints and boxes, while rails on the wall hold pens, stamps, and tape.

Double-Desk Duty

Having two work surfaces is helpful for separating computer and noncomputer work. Carrie uses this floating white table to spread out printer proofs and other large-format work she's reviewing.

Use **Walls (and Wall Coverings)** to Define Your Space

If you find yourself squeezing a work zone into another room, consider a few ways to make it feel more focused by visually differentiating it from the rest of the space.

Use an accent wall.

Paint and other wall coverings can help distinguish a specific area of a room. Sarah and Peter love old records, so they used this wallpaper that's designed to look like a vinyl collection in the desk area at the top of their stairs. The added interest helps it feel less like a hallway and more like room.

survey says: 46% of the people we polled have a desk or a work space within another room (most often the living room or guest bedroom).

Add (or fake) a wall.

When Mike and Lisa wanted a small work nook in the corner of their kitchen, they had a wall built to keep the work clutter out of sight from the casual eating area on the other side of the room. A tall bookcase would also do the trick if adding a wall isn't in the cards.

Don't Go **Overboard**

Home offices don't have to be covered in magnet boards, corkboards, chalkboards, and dry-erase boards. (Did we miss any? surfboards?) We're fans of those, but ask yourself if you really need them before filling your walls. You might find an alternative solution without sacrificing any productivity.

Pack in personality.
Choose art and objects that make you smile and keep you motivated, like Susan did in her garage-turned–home office. Simple frames keep a wide range of prints and posters looking clean instead of cluttered. She even worked in a large mirror for a view of the window behind her.

Add a fresh spin.
Susan has a lively meeting space behind her desk. To fit its un-corporate feel, she turned an old door into a leaning chalkboard and found a floating glass panel online that acts as a dry-erase board during meetings but is nearly invisible when it's not in use.

Stick It to **Something Different**

Magnets, pushpins, and tape work on all sorts of surfaces, so why feel bound to boards sold in the office aisle?

Keep it tray cool.

For a more modern spin, we combined a graphic tray and washi tape to make a high-impact "happy board" (you can fill it with favorite cards and notes or tape up gift cards and receipts you don't want to lose). A small sawtooth hanger added to the back makes it quick to hang, and the lip also becomes a ledge for bonus storage.

Try something old.

Hit up an architectural salvage shop or a thrift store for an interesting piece of wood, which will add more character to your work space than your run-of-the-mill corkboard. Here, we used T-pins to create a cool spot for mementos.

TIP

This tray is a HomeGoods find, but you can get the look by painting or stenciling a plain one too!

A Work Loft Made from Scratch

Allison and Jeremy
live with
Zulu (the dog)
and describe their suburban home as
Comfortable, Small, and Ours

Allison and Jeremy love their 800-square-foot home, but the small space leaves very little extra room to indulge in their hobbies and grow their business. (Allison runs an Etsy shop.) So they thought outside the box—er, walls—and built a large two-story garage from scratch with their own four hands, giving Jeremy room to tinker downstairs and earning Allison a large work area in the loft above.

Movin' On Up

Allison sells vinyl house numbers (which we coincidentally used in our first book), and she used to hole up in a spare bedroom to cut orders. She loves having a dedicated cutting area in the loft, and this orange rolling cart stores all of her vinyl, so it can be wheeled out whenever she needs it.

Sew Much Better

To fuel her sewing hobby, Allison created this simple sewing station on a spare wall. "I used to sew at our kitchen table, but I would have to put the machine away and wouldn't get back to it for months. Now my equipment stays in one place and all I have to do is flip a switch, so I'm more likely to jump into a new project."

I like to scratch!

Break Space

Even though the loft was intended primarily as a work space, it has also played host to family gatherings (like a recent baby shower), and Allison envisions it as a play space when she and Jeremy eventually have children. This built-in daybed under one window gives it a homey feel, and the reclaimed maple floors they laid themselves also help distinguish it from the industrial-looking concrete floors in the garage below.

This big flat file doubles as a coffee table with storage to spare!

Add a Surprise to Your Seat

Remember when the host of a show would say, "Now reach under your seat to find out what you've won!"? Well, this project isn't going to win you a prize, but it will have you sitting pretty. We found this wood secretary desk chair at a thrift store for five dollars. The paint was chippy, and we wanted to have a little fun, so after repainting the chair white (and shining its old brass casters), we decoupaged the top of the seat with pink pineapple wrapping paper from Spoonflower and some Mod Podge. After it dried, we topped the chair with a couple coats of clear water-based polyurethane sealer and it was ready for action.

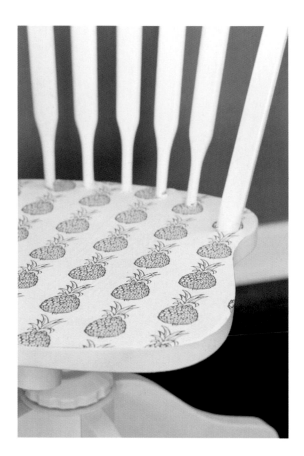

Create Cohesion with Finishes

Using pieces that share similar finishes but are otherwise different can bring a cohesive but not too matched feeling into a room. In her spare bedroom–turned-office, Christi pulled together white, gold, and navy items—even when it meant spray painting the gold details herself.

1 WHITE AND GOLD DRESSER. Christi customized a white Ikea dresser by adding gold-wrapped knobs and modern legs that she found online to make it more special.

2 NAVY AND WHITE CURTAINS. Christi selected the fabric for these curtains both for the color scheme and for the graphic pattern they add to the room.

3 GOLD AND NAVY STOOL. This store-bought stool got the gold-spray-paint treatment on the previously black legs, while Christi re-covered the top in fabric she liked (found on a pillow, of all places).

4 WHITE CHAIR. Not every piece in the room needs to feature more than one finish, like the sculptural secondhand desk chair, which remained all white.

Flexible Frames
Christi pulled the glass out of these frames so she could pin her daughter's artwork in them. Now she can easily swap the art out when she wants to update it.

Take **Cues** from the **Clipboard**

If you're one of those people who frames photos and never gets around to updating them (aren't we *all* that person?), you can get out from under the glass by creating this clipboard-style frame instead. The clips allow you to swap out reminders of whatever motivates you—whether it's a family portrait or a snapshot from a trip.

1 Cut a 1-by-12-inch **board** into 13-inch lengths (we made two).

2 Apply **stain** to your cut boards with a **paintbrush**. (We used a mixture of Minwax Dark Walnut and Classic Gray and applied a wood conditioner first for added grain and richness.)

3 After around five minutes, wipe the excess stain off with a **clean rag** and let everything dry. Finish the boards with a coat of **polyurethane sealer** if you'd like.

4 Once the boards have dried, use a **heavy-duty adhesive** like Super Glue to adhere two **magnet clips** to the board, near the top corners.

5 Attach two **sawtooth hangers** to the back and hang it on the wall with **nails**.

6 Clip up 8-by-10-inch photos or art. You can add dimension to the story your pictures tell by clipping up souvenirs, foreign currency, plane tickets, or other reminders of your adventures.

A Pool Room–Turned–Jewelry Studio

Karyn and Eric
live with
Memore (the dog) and Luna (the cat)
and describe their farmhouse as
Loved, Homey, and Cattywampus

When Karyn moved into her now-husband's 1940s farmhouse, he had a pool table in the sunroom and she had no place to build her jewelry business. You can probably see where this is going. With a clear vision for a cottage-like work space, Eric helped Karyn convert the sunroom into a studio where she can work and sell things without moving his pool table.

Up Above
Karyn's jewelry making involves the smoky process of soldering, so she and Eric converted an unused attic right above her sunroom work space into a studio to keep the smell (and the dust that flies) contained.

1 **BLUE SKIES AND WHITEWASH.** To give the log cabin-y room a lighter feel, they painted the ceiling a quiet blue and whitewashed the wood walls. Eric simply watered down some latex paint and brushed on a few thin coats.

2 **PUTTING THE POOL TABLE TO WORK.** Since Karyn sometimes hosts clients who are shopping for her designs, a place to spread out her work was a must. Simply covering the pool table with wood and fabric turned out to be a perfect solution.

Casual Lighting
To give her more light, Karyn deconstructed a 1980s chandelier and restrung the crystals haphazardly along with some big string lights.

Go **Wall to Wall**

Floor-to-ceiling bookcases or cabinets are particularly useful in offices where every inch counts. Beyond adding architectural interest to a boxy room, they also help contain your work stuff and better define your productivity zone, so that your office reference materials and supplies are less likely to take over a nearby living or sleeping space.

Cozy it up.
Wood-toned bookcases can lend a library vibe to any space. They are perfect for Andrew's home office, since he's a meticulous collector of books and baseball memorabilia. They also create a nice nook for a fold-out sofa bed since this space also doubles as a guest room.

Blend it in.

Katja and Frank installed shallow closed cabinets around the desk space within their guest bedroom. The concealed storage and white color palette keep the work space from feeling cluttered or busy since they can easily stash things away when visitors are staying.

PLAYING SPACES

John says

I HAVE A VERY DISTINCT MEMORY of when Sherry and I introduced a play area to our home for the first time. I'm not talking about the nursery or other baby items we set up when Clara arrived. I mean the space we needed when Clara finally was old enough to sit and have fun with something other than her own foot.

We proudly broke out the blocks, stuffed animals, and baby chew toys (or whatever you call them) that had been waiting for their moment to finally be interacted with. We spread them out in front of Clara on the thick, cushy living room rug that we'd purchased specifically with this moment in mind and waited for play to happen.

Clara's deep closet doubles as a bonus play area, which helps to contain tiny dollhouse items and other our-son-could-eat-that objects.

Honestly, I don't remember the next part—the part I probably should remember—that moment when Clara actually played with her toys and felt at home in her play space. No, what sticks out in my memory the most was the cleanup. We had purchased a large woven basket to house her toys in the living room so we could just quickly throw them in, toss a pretty blanket on top, and achieve covert toy storage.

Cleanup was so easy. So fast. So painless that Sherry and I were exchanging mental high fives. We had just won parenting, right? I wondered why people made such a big deal over kids' toys when we had somehow mastered it on our first try. We were writing for a parenting website at the time, so we even documented our slam dunk in a blog post. It's actually the photo we took of her toy pile that makes this moment so vivid in my brain.

Nearly five years later, that photo is ridiculously laughable to us—now that we have a greater appreciation for what a true toy mess can actually look like.

The Clara back then wasn't crawling yet, so the toy "pile" we were once so proud of wrangling was like six objects, spread out no farther than her little arms could reach from a stationary sitting spot. If that was a mess to us then, I'd hate to hear what old John and Sherry would say about the toy tornadoes we regularly experience these days.

Ah yes, the toys have gotten more plentiful, more spread out, and much smaller (and more painful to step on: I'm looking at you, Legos and tiny doll heels), so staying on top of them is a daily war, one that we don't always win, but hey, we try. And gone is the innocence of that first moment of play in our house . . . although not gone are those baskets, which we still swear by!

Let's give it up for baskets!

Making Way for Play

Like work, play happens in a variety of places in the average home. In fact, only one-third of the 35,000 folks we surveyed reported having a dedicated playroom. So most families find themselves carving out spots for toys and games elsewhere and—as it often feels around here—everywhere.

To us, that's not a bad thing. We're not trying to disguise the presence of children in our house. Sure, sometimes we could use a bit more picking up after ourselves, but ultimately we want Clara and Teddy to feel at home.

Whether parents want their kids to play nearby in order to keep tabs on them or just to enjoy their company, we spotted play spaces that are incorporated into all sorts of rooms and nooks in the homes we visited.

Fold-Away Play Zone
Lisa and Mike's basement play area also needed to host guests. Building in this Murphy bed was a great solution—and the wood planks they added to the bed's bottom lend warmth and interest when it's folded away.

Casual Art Corner

Keeping kid stuff in a room where you spend lots of time is always a smart move. Like this art table between Joey and Jeff's living room and kitchen, which inspired a playful gallery wall that's easily enjoyed during meal prep.

Fun Within **Reach**

Want to encourage more playtime under your roof? Here are some quick ideas for keeping play stuff easy to access *and* easy to live with.

✳ Try storing board games somewhere in your dining room (like in an existing built-in or buffet) to encourage post-dinner fun while you're all still gathered at the table.

✳ Keep a yard of vinyl fabric or oilcloth rolled up in your pantry or coat closet for a quick way to convert your kitchen table or island into an easy-to-wipe-up craft or art space.

✳ Storage pieces can be serious on the outside and still be full of fun inside. As long as it has drawers, shelves, or doors—like this secondhand armoire (left)— it can become toy storage in whatever room needs it.

✳ When buying a media cabinet or a coffee table, choose something with concealed storage; there are lots of options with lower drawers or even hidden compartments on top to wrangle video games and wireless remotes.

✳ Got Jack and Jill–style bedrooms upstairs? Consider splitting up functions instead of siblings. Paris and Arden are close enough in age that their parents turned one bedroom into a restful shared sleeping room and the other room into this toy and art space (opposite).

How We **Benched** Our Toys

After studying some expensive toy storage options, we came across this discounted entryway bench that gave us an idea. It was meant to store things like gloves and shoes, but we realized that adding a grid of shelves on top would give Clara a spot for everything from Legos and dolls to books and, well, more books. Here's how to do something similar.

✳ **START WITH A SMART BASE.** The versatility of the bench is what first caught our eye. The slide-in baskets can be removed for easier cleanup, while the fixed drawers offer a tailored look.

✳ **ADD A BOXED TOP.** We built a simple gridded bookshelf so Clara could access her library better (her previous system was a basket that was often dumped out in search of one book). We made this 13-by-13-inch cubby system with MDF, wood

glue, and nails, but there are similar store-bought solutions that would also work if you don't want to build something. Just be sure they are no wider or deeper than your bench.

✳ **FINISH WITH A FRESH COAT OF PAINT.** The original bench was off-white, so after securing our new top, we brightened it up and unified the two pieces by priming and then painting the whole thing in Simply White by Benjamin Moore.

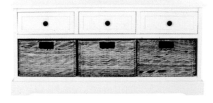

Misting the baskets with a pearlescent gold spray paint helped tie in the quirky mismatched knobs that Clara picked for the drawers.

Four Ways to Enjoy **Kid Art**

Kids' art is often just as cute as it is abundant. While every creation deserves to be appreciated, it often poses a storage and display challenge for those of us not planning to open a gallery anytime soon. Temporary display options like corkboards or clipboards allow you to rotate in new masterpieces easily, but even that isn't always enough to celebrate the most prolific of child Picassos. So here are four other ideas to consider.

1 IRON IT ON. Scan or photograph the artwork, then print it onto iron-on transfer paper, which is sold at most craft stores. Once the picture is printed, trim off any white space around your design (otherwise you'll see that telltale rectangular shape of the paper on your fabric later). Our daughter, Clara, picked this bunny she painted and we added it to a white throw pillow cover for her bed.

2 SHAPE IT. Assuming that taking scissors to your kid's art won't illicit tears from the artiste (Clara loves cutting hers up!), consider framing a big collection of pieces cut into fun new shapes. Basic squares or circles work, but we got playful by cutting them into a Popsicle shape and mounting each atop a mini Popsicle stick. Clara loved doing this project— and requested a real Popsicle at the end.

(continued)

1

2

3 MAT IT. If your child is still in the "abstract" phase of his artistic journey, you can layer his creations behind a mat to turn them into meaningful objects. We used a craft knife to cut a tropical fish shape out of card stock and placed it over some scribbles. Plus, you can swap in a new backdrop whenever your mini Monet churns one out.

4 CATALOG IT. Ultimately, most of us don't have the space to save every doodle. And our best efforts to stuff binders are often thwarted by oversized or 3D creations. That's why we began digitally documenting everything with an app called Artkive. We snap pics of the pieces, and it keeps them all in an album on our phones. At the end of the year, we print them in a slim photo book, complete with funny captions dictated by the artist herself.

TIP

Picture this.
To capture great
shots of your child's art,
choose a simple back-
ground that you can use
every time—like a white
tabletop. Try to photograph
things when the light is
bright, but not shining
directly on the art.

"That's my monster from Art Camp!"

"Such a colorful bunny house. Bunnies lives there."

"This is an octopus named Spider. She is scared of sharks."

"This is a rainbow at my house. It's beautiful."

Small-Space Surprises

If you're tight on areas for play in your home, sometimes even a small wall or corner can create big fun for your little ones.

Make a hideout under the stairs.
Nicole and Jason carved out a play area there for their kids since they couldn't work a full-sized playroom into the floor plan. It's cozy enough to feel special, but large enough for Mom to join in the action, and they love having another spot to stash toys.

Create costume central.
Courtney and Jack kept this collection of dress-up clothes from collecting dust in a bin by hanging them on simple hooks in their daughter's room. It makes it easier for the kids to see the outfits and put them away when they're done playing with them.

Add a secret tunnel.
When Courtney and Jack were having a doorway added to connect two rooms on their first floor, they had the idea to do something similar but shrunken where their son's closet adjoined his sister's room. The affectionately named "mouse hole" has become a favorite way for the siblings to play together, and at night the closet door gets closed so there's no sneaking around.

Hang Up a Few **Traditions**

Who doesn't love a family tradition? Here's how we got two of them up on the walls at our house.

1 GROWTH GRID. We took weekly photos of our kids laying on colorful fabric backgrounds to document their growth during their first year of life. We loved the results so much it felt sad to just tuck them away in boxes or albums. So we ordered custom prints from Social Print Studio, a site that automatically arranges your favorite snapshots into a grid. The results are colorful and meaningful, and they fit easily into 20-by-30-inch frames we bought online. Grids like these are also great for a collection of first-day-of-school photos, pictures from a family vacation, or, of course, your favorite Instagrams.

2 CLOCK TIME. We made a clock for our daughter, Clara, a few years ago using a craft store clock kit, so we thought it would be a fun tradition to continue for our son, Teddy. Since his sister nicknamed him "Barnacle," we decided a sea creature was in order, and we soon found this whale-shaped cutting board on Etsy. We drilled a hole to accommodate the clock kit and added simple white number stickers. Teddy's not going to be telling time for a while, but we're all enjoying the new wall addition. You could use other cutting board or craft wood shapes as your clock base, or even cut your own with a jigsaw and some plywood (painting it is optional too!).

Creating a Homework Zone

Lois and Peter
live with
**Hannah-Louise (age 8), GiGi (age 5), Georgia (the dog),
and Mr. Gills and Mr. Andrew (the fish)**
and describe their home as
Warm, Cheerful, and a Tad Crazy

Devoting a spot in your house to the kids doesn't necessarily mean it needs to foster high-energy (and high-volume) activities. When their older daughter started getting homework assignments, Lois and Peter found that the open floor plan on their first floor was "a nightmare" (think folders, papers, and distractions everywhere). So they converted a spare bedroom into a "homework room" so both girls would have a calm space where they could focus and keep their papers corralled.

Lend a learning vibe.

A huge set of classroom maps that Lois found in a secondhand shop helps to establish the homework vibe of the room. Not only is it a great reference for the girls, but it also conveniently covers a magnetic-paint mishap on the back wall.

Go fish.

Lois and Peter had a local carpenter build the bookshelves around the window, including the bench seat with hidden storage. Knowing they wanted to put a fish tank on one of the shelves (at a level where the girls could easily interact with it), they smartly had that shelf reinforced to hold the weight of the water. Instead of resting it on adjustable pegs, the carpenter screwed it in using heavy-duty brackets.

Stretch Your Homework Organization

WEEKEND PROJECT

Did you know that craft stores sell bungee cords? And that they come in tons of colors? We snagged a couple to wrangle some stuff that a young scholar might want on hand for an afternoon of hitting the books. It's nice to get a few things off the ol' desktop.

1 Cut a sheet of ¾-inch **plywood** to your desired size (ours was 2 by 4 feet wide). We used our table saw, but most home-improvement stores will cut purchases for you.

2 Cut a 2-inch strip off of the bottom of your plywood (decreasing the height, not the length). This will become the bottom ledge.

3 Lay out the items you want to organize on your board and plan where you'll want to thread the **bungee cord**.

4 Mark those spots with a **pencil** and use a **drill** fitted with a ³⁄₁₆-**inch bit** to make holes at each mark. Sand the holes smooth and test each to be sure your bungee cord slides through easily.

5 Prime and paint the entire board and shelf piece using a **small foam roller** (and a paintbrush if needed).

6 Once the board is dry, you can begin attaching the shelf. Run a bead of

wood glue across the back edge of the shelf board, and then hold it tightly against the bottom edge of the large board, forming a right angle. Secure with **2-inch screws** through the back. You may need a helper for this step.

7 To begin adding your bungees, thread one end through the front of your first hole and knot it tightly on the back of the board. Repeat with the other end in the next hole, leaving enough slack for

(continued)

the desired item to fit (keep in mind, it stretches!) Cut off any excess in the back with scissors. We had fun alternating cord colors and making different shapes with them.

8 Once all of your bungee cords are added, nail two large sawtooth hangers onto the back of the board near either end of the top edge. These will rest on screws that go into a stud or a heavy-duty anchor in your wall.

9 Have fun hanging items, using the ledge to rest books and heavier objects. Also consider adding cups to hold small supplies like pencils, highlighters, or flash drives. Now study up!

Meaningful Minis

We seem to accumulate small treasures that end up in random boxes and corners—so this antique letterpress tray from Etsy helps us get them up on the wall where we can all enjoy them. The compartments are the perfect size for the heart-shaped rocks and other trinkets we've gathered (and painted) with Clara over the years, and they're a lot more soak-up-able when they're not shoved in a box somewhere. We carefully removed the back panel and painted it blue to help the objects inside stand out a little more, and we hung the drawer on the wall with two sawtooth hangers that we added to the back.

Color Their World

Play spaces are a great excuse to have fun with color (the goal is fun, after all). But before you let loose, here are some tips to keep the room from going from cheerful to psychedelic crazytown.

* Colors that look "bright" on paint swatches can be super neon on the wall, so one of our favorite tips is to choose a swatch with a slightly gray, muted undertone, which should still look plenty vibrant on the wall. (To avoid any mishaps, paint on some test swatches before committing.)

* Many larger-scale toys or playsets are colorful, so it helps to assess your stockpile (you know, what's going into the room) before choosing the colors for the room. That can help you avoid anything that might clash or get too crazy.

* White or neutral walls might seem too boring for a playroom, but they often allow you the most flexibility for bright items like colorful rugs, furnishings, window treatments, art, and even a softly toned ceiling.

* Adding in some natural elements (a wood-toned bookcase, a sisal rug, some storage baskets) can temper bright colors and bring balance.

* If the play space is part of a child's bedroom, keep in mind the restful functions (like sleep or studying) that room should meet as well before committing to a color.

Not Too Blue
Thanks to the large windows and neutral furnishings, the vibrant teal walls that Eames has in his room are playful without feeling overwhelming.

Make **Toy Boxes** (Literally)

Storage boxes are great additions for containing small clutter and supplies on desktops or bookshelves. Try dressing up a basic wooden craft box with an extra—or thrifted!—toy, like a matchbox car, animal figurine, or action figure. Some heavy-duty glue and a unifying coat of spray paint will do the trick (we used army green for these army men).

Age this up.
Steal this idea for your grown-up spaces too by swapping out playthings for pretty things, like a decorative stone or a sparkly cabinet knob (and feel free to skip the spray paint).

Get **Sew Sweet**

Another cute addition to our play space is this two-dollar embroidery hoop we customized with a just-home-from-the-hospital photo of Teddy that we printed on transfer paper. Once the picture was ironed on to plain white fabric and fitted in the hoop, we stitched a simple, playful design around his little face using thread. Then our hearts melted all over again. You can lean it on a shelf, hang it on the wall, or even make smaller versions to use as Christmas ornaments.

Pick a Kid-Friendly
Floor Covering

Having something comfortable underfoot can be a big plus, but the fear of spills and stains can make the idea of carpet somewhat scary. Our favorite solution is an area rug to warm up a wood or tile floor (it can even work over carpeting to help define a zone). There are lots of durable, kid-friendly (and dog-friendly! and klutzy adult–friendly!) materials that offer a range of price and pattern options too.

1 TUFTED WOOL RUG

Pro: Usually the thickest, softest, and arguably most upscale option, plus natural fibers typically respond well to stain cleanup and are known to last

Con: Wool rugs with an especially high pile can create a haven for crumbs and dirt to hide, and wool can get pretty pricey

2 FLAT-WEAVE RUG

Pro: Typically made of wool or cotton, they boast the same natural-fiber cleanup as tufted rugs, but the thinner profile helps keep the price down—especially when buying larger sizes

Con: Lightweight, thin designs mean rug pads are needed to add cushioning and keep things in place (anchoring with furniture helps too)

3 JUTE OR SISAL RUG

Pro: Often the most wipeable natural fiber option, plus it lends a neutral color and casual texture that you may not find in other choices

Con: Some can be too scratchy feeling, so it helps to test them in person or read online reviews before buying

This tightly woven jute rug was a low-stress addition to the kids' rooms in Abby and Tait's beachy vacation home.

4 INDOOR/ OUTDOOR RUG

Pro: Many look and feel like natural-fiber rugs, but the synthetic material is often durable enough to be hosed off or even bleached

Con: Cheaper versions can have a plastic look or feel, and some may off-gas or have a chemical smell that can make buying online risky

5 CARPET TILES

Pro: These offer great design and size flexibility, as well as the option to replace a single stained or damaged tile

Con: They're thinner and stiffer than traditional rugs, providing less softness for falls, and can also get pretty pricey, depending on your preferences

6 FOAM TILES

Pro: Similar to carpet tiles, but completely wipeable and with unbeatable impact absorption for little ones

Con: Hard to integrate into adult spaces since most versions are sold only in bright, primary colors

Sidhya found wood-look foam tiles online, which help the playroom visually coexist with the adjacent living area.

Corral a **Collection**

We both had key chain collections as kids, so it shouldn't have surprised us when Clara was drawn to them too. (Maybe it's in our blood?) Clara's collection started during our first book tour, when we bought them for her in each city we visited, and it has grown as we've hit new landmarks, museums, and other attractions together over the years.

Our childhood collections usually lived in a box or a tangled clump, so we wanted a more functional and fun way for Clara to enjoy hers—a designated spot where they could be admired, accessed, and added to over time. The solution ended up being simple: two wall hooks and a 1-inch-thick wooden dowel from Home Depot that we cut down into two 12-inch sections. The wooden rod can be lifted off the hooks, allowing the key chains to slide free so Clara can add to her collection or play with them, but when they're "put away" on the wall, they can still be enjoyed instead of hidden away and forgotten.

Adapt It.
This also works for organizing necklaces, bracelets, medals, belts, watches, or ties—and a smaller dowel could hold rings and dangly earrings.

Take Things **Outside**

If it feels like your house just can't handle any more chaos, there's always the great outdoors. Sara and Jason created a fun-filled playhouse for their son and daughter using money inherited from Sara's grandmother, making the space as meaningful as it is awesome. Here are some of the things that contribute to its charm.

✳ **INTERACTIVE ADDITIONS.** As a family, they gave their playhouse features like a Dutch door (complete with a chalkboard on the back) and window boxes that the kids can plant with flowers themselves.

✳ **SPILLOVER SPACE.** The playhouse essentially creates a bonus playroom, complete with a small pretend kitchen and a tiny worktable.

✳ **FRESH AIR.** Not only does this give the kids a little home of their own to take care of—from sweeping it out to watering the flowers—it also gets them out of the house, which is always a nice change of scenery.

Circle of Friends

Sometimes it feels like a miracle that our daughter doesn't drown in stuffed animals. (Seriously, how is there room in the bed for her?!) So if you've got someone who is similarly plush-obsessed, try finding those fluffy friends a new (but not *too* far away) home, thanks to a set of cardboard hatboxes.

1 Determine your arrangement of **hatboxes** on the floor first. Since the set we bought at Jo-Ann Fabric and Crafts included varying sizes, a random layout worked best.

2 Place each hatbox on a **drop cloth,** grouping those that will be painted the same color. We painted ours with Rust-Oleum Seaside, Lagoon, and Candy Pink.

3 Spray all sides (except the bottom) with thin, even coats. It may soak into the cardboard, so a second coat will likely be needed.

4 Once the hatboxes are dry, hang them on your wall with a **nail** through the middle of each one and load 'em up!

CONCLUSION

ONE OF THE COOLEST PARTS of writing this book was talking with dozens of families and realizing that we're all in the same boat. Well, actually, our metaphorical boats are wildly different—there are endless combinations of floor plans, families, budgets, and styles—but we're all just trying to do the best we can. While we hope these pages have given you ideas, tips, and inspiration to make the most of your home, what we also hope is that you are encouraged to embrace the imperfection that is real life. No matter how perfect a house may seem from the outside or in photos (even ours and the ones featured in this book), every home has its shortcomings, its messes, and its rooms that aren't exactly what we dream for them to be. So let's all try to stress a little less, kick up our heels a little more, and enjoy these places that we call home.

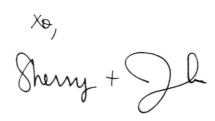

xo,

Sherry + John

THANK YOU

Why do these thank-you blurbs always make our eyes leak? It's just kind of a crazy thing, to watch scribbles, ideas, photos, and a whole bunch of words grow into a book—this tangible thing you can hold and read and smell (gotta smell a book). We never thought we could love another book like our first one, but it turns out that much like children, your heart expands to make room. So we're sending out a huge thank-you to Rachel Sussman, Judy Pray, Michelle Ishay-Cohen, Sibylle Kazeroid, Todd Wright, John Waters, and everyone else who helped us birth this second book baby of ours. Of course we wouldn't be anywhere without our amazing friends, who keep us laughing (shout-out to Cat, Travis, Heather, Lesley, Katie, Jeremy, KK, Matt, Julia, Dana, Kevin, Michael, and John's neighborhood running posse); the entire design community (bloggers, designers, authors, and more), which keeps us inspired; and our wonderful family (especially our moms and dads), who love us—and feed us—no matter what (we're raising a giant chocolate turkey in your honor . . . and then eating it). We'd also never be here without our beloved blog readers, who dropped in on us for all those amazing years of sharing our life and our home with the interwebs, so there's a big bear hug coming your way. Nope not a friendly handshake or a fist bump. Get ready for some serious personal-space invasion. They say gratitude makes what you have enough, and our cup runneth over.

SOURCE LIST

sectional: Ikea; rug: overstock.com; door color: Onyx Black by Glidden

Page 63 Pink fireplace paint: Alcro Designers NCS S 0515-R20B; candlesticks: Lagerhaus; bookcase: Craigslist

Page 65 Chairs, rug: secondhand; curtains: Pottery Barn; pillows, lamp: HomeGoods

Page 67 Photo 1: Coffee table, bentwood chairs: thrift store; blue sofa, arc lamp: LaDiff; Photo 2: Bed: discontinued; door screen: homemade; Photo 3: Table: secondhand; rug: Nomadic Trading; clock: family heirloom

Page 73 Sofa: Ikea; pillows: Target; drop cloth curtains: Home Depot

EATING SPACES

Page 74 Bamboo blinds, pendant light: Home Depot; floating shelves: Ikea; faux clamshell: ZGallerie; counters: Ardex; white cabinet color: Simply White by Benjamin Moore

Page 79 Island: secondhand; floor pattern: homemade; chandelier: antique: cabinet color: London Stone by Farrow & Ball

Page 80 Hardware: Pottery Barn; clock: Ikea

Page 81 Fabric: Michael Miller Bekko Home Decor Swell in Navy; duck head: secondhand

Page 83 Wood frame: Target; black-and-white art: Kate Horne

Page 85 Floating shelves: reclaimed wood with Ikea brackets

Page 87 Pot rack: homemade; backsplash shelves: Ikea

Page 90 Mugs: HomeGoods and Target

Pages 93–94 Pendant lights: Circa Lighting; stools: West Elm;

upholstered bench: custom; backsplash tile: Daltile; island color: Knoxville Gray by Benjamin Moore

Page 96 Wood chairs, table: hand-me-down; chandelier: Lindsey Adelman; vases: HomeGoods

Page 97 Light: Shades of Light; silhouette art: Gibson Lane Studio

Page 101 Pendant lights: Ballard Designs; orange paint for lights: Paprika by Rust-Oleum

Page 102 Backsplash tile: Skyline Vein Cut by Marble Systems; blue range: Viking

Page 103 Stools: secondhand; CD rack turned towel holder: Ikea

Page 105 Stools: Modernica; pendant lights: amazon.com

Page 106 Pendant lights: Schoolhouse Electric; woven chair: TJ Maxx; towel bar: Lowe's

Page 107 Accent tile: Mosaic Tile Company; teakettle: Cost Plus World Market

Page 109 Farmhouse sink, pendant lights, metal shelf brackets: Ikea; faucet: Lowe's

Pages 110–11 Metal farmhouse sink, faucet: Etsy; shelves, counters, pull-out island: homemade

Page 113 Metal island: Retail Resource; stools: overstock.com; bamboo blinds: Home Depot

Page 117 Table, chairs: hand-me-down; chandelier: Schonbek; rug: Joss & Main; bathroom wallpaper: Bramble by Laura Ashley

Pages 118–21 Chandelier, succulent art, candlestick: West Elm; buffet, wood chairs: Craigslist; rug: Amir Rugs; bamboo blinds: Home Depot; vase, rhino: ZGallerie

Page 124 Table, blue chairs: West Elm; ghost chairs: Amazon

Page 125 Table: Restoration Hardware; chairs: All Modern; curtains: Ikea; rug: FLOR; vase: Target

Page 127 Left photo: Wood table, chairs: Restoration Hardware; chandelier: Circa Lighting; Right photos: Wallpaper: Williams & Sherrill; art: Claiborne Riley; table: Mr. Brown (with custom top); chairs: Restoration Hardware; chandelier: Arteriors

Page 129 Chandelier: Ruth & Ollie; chairs, table: hand-me-downs; rug: Madeline Weinrib; curtain fabric: Williams & Sherrill; hourly decorating consultant: Claiborne Riley

SLEEPING SPACES

Page 130 Lamps: HomeGoods; nightstands, rug: Joss & Main; frames: Michaels; duvet: Ikea; headboard: homemade; yellow pillows: Dermond Peterson; wall color: Black Pepper by Benjamin Moore

Page 132 Duvet, chandelier: West Elm; bed, white curtains: Ikea; tan curtains: Bed Bath & Beyond; sconces: Lamp Factory Outlet; rug: Cost Plus World Market; wall color: Gentle Tide by Glidden

Page 135–37 Sconces: The Decorating Outlet; mirror: Cost Plus World Market; patterned shams, rug: Pottery Barn; sheets: Target; duvet: Ikea; bolster pillow: HomeGoods

Page 139 Wallpaper: Williams & Sherrill; headboard: custom made; lamp: Restoration Hardware; nightstand: West Elm

Page 140 Nightstand: Target; floral sham: Pottery Barn; duvet: Ikea; lamp: Linens 'n Things; wall color: Sparrow by Benjamin Moore

Page 143 Mirror: hand-me-down; pink rug: antique

Page 144 Table: flea market; basket: Ikea; lamp: HomeGoods

Page 145 Nightstand: hand-me-down; nightstand paint color: Americana by Benjamin Moore; sconce: Arteriors

Pages 148–49 Red beds: Walmart; dresser, art above dresser, dining table, dining chairs: Craigslist; photo mural, bookcases: Ikea; arc lamp: West Elm

Page 150 Mirror: West Elm; rug: Dash & Albert; bed, dresser: Green Front Furniture; art: Lesli DeVito

Pages 152–53 White vanity: thrift store; leather closet pulls: LeeValley.com

Page 154 Wall hooks: vintage; rhino wall hanging: TJ Maxx; green quilt: homemade

Page 157 Door color: Irish Moss by Benjamin Moore; play kitchen: homemade

Page 159 Wallpaper: Anthropologie; headboard, bedding: Target; lamp: Home Depot; suitcases: thrift store

Pages 160–61 Chandelier: Ikea; pink lamp: Robert Abbey; window treatments: custom made; ceiling color: Impatience Petal by Sherwin-Williams

Page 162 Stencil: Royal Design Studio; red birdcage: thrift store; dresser: Craigslist; moose lamp: estate sale; blue fan: amazon.com; "C" on door: Anthropologie; rug: The Decorating Outlet; bowl: Ikea (we painted it blue and red)

Page 167 Lettered duvet, white chair: Ikea; wood shelves: homemade; accent wall color: Blue Coal by Valspar

Pages 170–71 Sconce: West Elm Outlet; mobile: vintage find; mural

paint colors (top to bottom): Tricorn Black, Citrine, Overt Green, and Garden Spot by Sherwin-Williams

Pages 172–73 Curtain fabric: Annalee Brickwalk Red/Pink; chandelier: Urban Outfitters; art: One Kings Lane; pink cow head: travel souvenir; hanging chair: Serena & Lily; rug: West Elm

WASHING SPACES

Page 176 Lights, cabinet hardware: Lowes; mirrors, yellow planter: HomeGoods; art: Lesli DeVito; towel hook: thrift store; wall and cabinet color: Simply White by Benjamin Moore

Page 178 Cabinets, under-cabinet lighting: Ikea; cabinet hardware: Lowe's; counters: homemade; backsplash tile, floor tile: The Tile Shop; green metal tins: Cost Plus World Market; laundry sorter: Crate & Barrel; wall color: Going to the Chapel by Benjamin Moore

Pages 181–83 Painting: chrislovesjulia.etsy.com; armadillo print: funnelcloud.etsy.com; basket, stool: HomeGoods; towel hook: Young House Love; hand towel: West Elm; wall color: Edgecomb Gray with Pearlescent Glaze

Page 186 Tub: York by Victoria + Albert; floor tile: The Tile Shop

Page 189 Wallpaper on left: Williams & Sherrill; wallpaper on right: Brocante Wallpaper by Pip Studio

Page 190 Mirrors: HomeGoods; wall color: Starless Night by Behr

Page 194 Vessel sink: faucetdirect.com; mirror: TJ Maxx

Page 195 Dresser: secondhand; sink: Habitat for Humanity ReStore; wall faucet, mirror: homemade

Page 196 Floor tile: Mosaic Tile Company; vanity color: Courtyard Green by Benjamin Moore

Page 199 Toilet: Kohler; pendant light: Lamps Plus; vessel sink: Ron Bow; wall faucet: Grohe

Pages 204–5 Table: Ikea; stools, green bins: Pottery Barn; rug: Layla Grace

ENTRY SPACES

Page 210 Star pendant: The Decorating Outlet; painting: Teil Duncan; wall color: Edgecomb Gray by Benjamin Moore; door color: Blue Lake by Benjamin Moore

Page 212 Painting: homemade; green buffet: Craigslist; curtain fabric: Robert Allen Khanjali Peacock from U-Fab; wall color: Moonshine by Benjamin Moore; door color: Full Sun by Valspar

Page 215 Shelf wood, metal brackets: Home Depot; clock, metal pear, basket, mirror, wood drawers: HomeGoods; dresser: Green Front Furniture; frames, letter B: Target

Pages 217–19 Bagged folding chairs, storage bin: Target; bin paint: Oil Rubbed Bronze by Rust-Oleum Universal; wall hooks: Liberty Hardware; welcome mat: West Elm; rubber stair treads: Improvements catalog; dark stair color: Urbane Bronze by Sherwin-Williams; door color: Blue Lake by Benjamin Moore

Page 221 Mirror with hooks: Pottery Barn; shoe rack: Ikea; door color: Blue Lake by Benjamin Moore

Page 225 Chandelier: hand-me-down; curtains: homemade; art: Claiborne Riley; chair: secondhand; round table: Ruth & Ollie; rug: Cost Plus World Market

Page 228 Console: West Elm; trunk and lamp: hand-me-downs

Page 229 Wooden cubby organizer: Pottery Barn; rug: FLOR; wall hooks: Home Depot

Page 230 Dresser: yard sale; art: secondhand; lamp: Target; wall hooks: Home Depot; metal bin: TJ Maxx

Page 232 Chandelier: Ferguson; door: DSA Doors; rug: antique; mail holder: secondhand; blue cabinet, coral, inlay box: HomeGoods

Page 235 Rug: Cost Plus World Market

Page 237 Wallpaper: Albert Hadley's Fireworks for Hinson & Co; art: Shepard Fairey via 1708 Gallery; entry table: Modern Artifacts

Page 238 Tea towels: fab.com

Page 239 Wallpaper: Waverly Country Life in Black; picture frames: Michaels

Page 240 Console table, basket: HomeGoods

Page 245 Stencil: Sunny Goode

Page 246 Bamboo chairs: secondhand; door color: Santa Monica Blue by Benjamin Moore

Page 247 Dog bed: Orvis; hardware: West Elm; brick floor: reclaimed

Pages 248–49 Dining set: secondhand; entry bench: West Elm; entry rugs: Target; coat hook: Herman Miller

Page 251 Chest: homemade; banister color: Restoration Hardware's Spanish Moss

WORKING SPACES

Page 252 Parsons desk: West Elm; desk chair: Pottery Barn Teen; art: Brenda Anderson; bookshelf, curtains: Ikea; bamboo blinds: Home Depot; floating desk: Craigslist; woven benches: Target; metallic

rug: Joss & Main; wall color: Palest Pistachio by Benjamin Moore

Page 255 Desk, corkboard: homemade; chairs: yard sale

Page 257 Desks, rug, white chairs: Ikea; red stool: hand-me-down

Page 259 Pendant light: Visual Comfort Lighting; desk: Ikea; chair: Ballard Designs; rug: West Elm

Page 260 Parsons desk: West Elm; desk chair: Pottery Barn Teen; lamp: HomeGoods; magnet board: homemade; wire basket: Target

Page 261 Lamp, wire tray: Target; desk: Green Front Furniture; yellow electrical tape: Home Depot

Page 263 Artwork: Sunny Goode; cowhide rug: Ikea

Page 265 Frames, drawer bases: Ikea; desktop: homemade; chair: Joss & Main; blue jug: Target; wall color: Sparrow by Benjamin Moore

Page 267 Pendant light: Circa Lighting; rug: Crate & Barrel; acrylic desk: Wisteria; gold frames: West Elm

Page 268 Rolling cabinets, frames, floating shelves: Ikea

Page 269 Both desks: Pottery Barn; curtains, yellow clock: Ikea

Page 270 Wallpaper: Record Shelf by Eco Wallpaper; bookshelves: Craigslist; desk: hand-me-down; floor lamp: secondhand

Page 271 Desk, shelves: built-in; chair: Ikea

Page 272 Pendant lights: Ikea; curtains: Ballard Designs; table, chairs, door: secondhand; glass whiteboard: Amazon

Page 273 Chair, large "C": secondhand; desk: Pottery Barn; basket: Target; tote bag: Need Supply Co.

Page 276 Orange rolling cart: homemade and painted Picante by Benjamin Moore; campaign desk: secondhand

Page 277 Daybed, tassel banner: homemade; bedding: Target; metal file: Craigslist

Page 279 Parsons desk: West Elm; drum stool: HomeGoods; wall color: Black Pepper by Benjamin Moore

Page 281 Curtain fabric: Mary Jo's; dresser, sheepskin rug, frames: Ikea; dresser hardware: Anthropologie; dresser legs: tablelegs.com; bench: Target; woven rug: FLOR; chair: secondhand; arrows in vase: Clic General Store

Pages 284–85 Chandelier: secondhand; jewelry: Karyn Shonk Designs

Page 286 Bookcases, desk: custom built; chair: vintage; chest: secondhand

Page 287 Built-ins, desk, chair: Ikea; rug: H&M; pouf: Target

PLAYING SPACES

Page 288 Curtains: Ikea (dyed pink); daybed, rug: West Elm; pouf: Joss & Main; table, peg cubby, clock, canopy, bookshelf: homemade; chairs: thrift store; name art: Numsi; bunny art: ZouZou's Basement

Page 290 Fabric: Peaceful Perch by Dena Home at U-Fab; dollhouse, painted basket: homemade; wall color: Cadillac Pink by Benjamin Moore; door color: Cinco de Mayo by Benjamin Moore

Page 291 Art: Public Bikes; frames: homemade; changing pad cover: modfox.etsy.com; bookcase: Ikea (framed in wood); animal bins, green box, green basket: Target; rug: HomeGoods; wall color: Going to the Chapel by Benjamin Moore

Page 292 Murphy bed: murphybeddepot.com; wood slats: homemade; red beanbag: FatBoy; play table: Ikea

Page 293 Play table: Ikea, daybed: built-in; pillow: Anthropologie

Page 295 Table, chairs, armoire, stool: secondhand; curtains: Mill Outlet Village; chandelier: eBay

Page 297 Bench: Joss & Main; round basket: HomeGoods; hardware: Anthropologie; Judy Garland art: Noah Scalin; Fierce quote art: Cat Coquillette; pink monster: homemade by Daisies and Crazies; octopus toy: philbarbato.etsy.com

Pages 300–301 Frame, towels: Target; photo book: MyPublisher

Page 305 Photo 1: Print: Social Print Studio; frame: Craig Frames

on amazon.com; Photo 2: clock kit: Michaels

Pages 306–7 Desk: Pottery Barn found via Craigslist; chairs, planter: HomeGoods; pendant light: The Decorating Outlet; rug: TJ Maxx; turtle stool: secondhand

Page 308 Bungee cords: JoAnn Fabric & Crafts; desk: Ikea; homework items, stool, robot bank: Target; classic books: thrift store

Page 313 Bookcase: secondhand; workbench: Melissa & Doug; rug: Ikea; wall color: Cloudburst by Sherwin-Williams

Page 314 Wood boxes: JoAnn Fabric & Crafts; army men: Target

Page 315 Embroidery hoop: JoAnn Fabric & Crafts; iron-on transfer paper: Target

Page 317 Woven rug: Overstock; play kitchen: Pottery Barn; foam tiles: Amazon

Page 318 Hooks: Home Depot (painted blue); curtains: Ikea (dyed pink); blue clock, book shelf, pom-pom canopy: homemade

Page 321 Playhouse: homemade; siding color: Olympic's Deep Charcoal Stain; door color: Sherwin-William's Brittlebrush

Page 323 Wall stencil: Royal Design Studio; stencil color: Hibiscus by Benjamin Moore; pink headboard: thrift store

CONCLUSION

Page 325 See sources for page 130

Wanna know where I got it? I got it from my mama.

A BIG SMOOCH
TO THE FAMILIES

(AND SOME PHOTO CREDITS)

We're so grateful to the families who so graciously invited us into their homes for this book. It wouldn't have been possible to explore how real families live without some generous families who shared their stories, challenges, and beautiful spaces with us. Below is a list of each family, along with the pages you can find their home featured on. (If they have a home-related website, that's listed too.) All photos are by Todd Wright unless otherwise noted on these pages.

Abby & Tait's Family / Seen on pages 33, 51 (bottom right), 144, 317 (left) / Photos by Abby Larson

Aletha & Greg's Family / Seen on pages 36, 104, 105, 248, 249, 313 / See more at www.midmodmich.com / Photos by Kristen Carlson, K. Holly Photography

Allison & Jeremy / Seen on pages 276, 277 / See more at jabaayave.wordpress.com / Photos by Allison Jabaay

Amber & Nick's Family / Seen on pages 170, 171 / See more at www.willscasa.com / Photos by Nick Wills

Amy & Graham's Family / Seen on pages 152, 159, 209, 239

Anna & Liam / Seen on pages 44, 89 (bottom left), 115 (top left) / See more at www.live-style.co.uk / Photos by Kirsten Robertson Photography

Carrie & Matt 's Family / Seen on pages 45, 125, 229, 238, 268, 269

Cate & Frank's Family / Seen on pages 53, 81 / Photos by Jordan Maunder Photography

Christi & Barrett's Family / Seen on pages 26, 27, 172, 173, 281 / Photos by Amy Free

Courtney & Jack's Family / Seen on pages 113, 124, 221, 302, 303

Elisabeth / Seen on pages 34, 35, 59 (bottom right), 228 / Photos by John Petersik

Emily & Shane / Seen on pages 51 (top left), 62, 96, 108,

109 / See more at www
.lifestyleanddesignonline.com /
Photos by Karl Poynter

Emily & Todd's Family / Seen
on pages 46, 61, 89 (top), 206,
230, 231, 257

Hillary & Scott's Family /
Seen on pages 46, 49 / See more
at www.friendly-home.net /
Photos by Hillary Dickman

Jamie & AJ's Family / Seen
on pages 72, 73 / See more at
www.jamiefinkdesigns.com /
Photos by Tony Skarlatos and
Denise Fink

Jenny & Jay's Family / Seen
on pages 39, 51 (top right),
97, 129, 189 (left), 225, 245 /
Photos by John Petersik

Jessica & Taylor's Family /
Seen on pages 160, 161 /
Photos by Amy Free

Joey & Jeff's Family / Seen on
pages 13 (top right), 41, 55, 60,
87, 115 (bottom left), 169, 193,
235, 243, 244, 293 / See more
at latitude38LLC.com/blog

Kai's Family / Seen on
pages 148, 149 / See
more at instagram.com/
theamazingchaos / Photos by
Kai Saunders

Karyn & Eric / Seen on pages
59 (top right), 192 (left), 284,
285

Katherine & Richard's
Family / Seen on pages 59
(left), 102, 127 (right), 139,
204, 205, 222, 223, 258, 259

Katja & Frank's Family / Seen
on pages 166–67, 199, 287 /
See more at shiftctrlart.com /
Photos by Katja Kromann

Lisa & Mike's Family / Seen
on pages 42, 54, 147, 271
(right), 292

Lois & Peter's Family / Seen
on pages 306, 307

Margarete & Kevin's Family /
Seen on pages 116, 117

Meg / Seen on pages 85, 250,
251

Megan & Greg's Family /
Seen on page 154 / See more
at thehomesihavemade.com /
Photos by Megan Duesterhaus

Monica & Dean's Family /
Seen on pages 40, 106, 107,
192, 294, 295

Nicole & Jason's Family /
Seen on pages 92–93, 94, 127
(left), 247, 266, 267, 302 (left) /
Designed by Marie Flanigan
Interiors / Photos by Julie
Soefer Photography

Sara & Jason's Family /
Seen on pages 69, 320, 321 /
See more at parcelandfrock
.blogspot.com / Photos by ISO
Photo Studio

Sarah & Peter's Family / Seen
on pages 63, 189 (right), 270,
271 (left) / Photos by Benita
Larsson

Sidhya & Maneesh's Family /
Seen on page 317 (right) /
Photo by pinkletoes.com

Sunny & Read's Family /
Seen on pages 37, 51 (bottom
left), 79, 80, 143, 145, 153,
246, 262, 263 / See more at
sunnygoode.com

Susan & Andrew / Seen on
pages 115 (top right), 187,
194, 236, 237, 272, 273, 286

Teeni & Trevor's Family /
Seen on pages 110, 111 /
Photos by Krystal Stuber

Wendy / Seen on pages 67,
103, 195 / Photos by John
Petersik

Additional Photo Credits

Pages 15, 264, 265, 278, 279,
311, 325 / Photos by John
Petersik

Pages 32, 296 / Images
courtesy of Joss & Main

Page 165 / Photo prints
courtesy of Sherri Conley

Page 215 / Family photos
courtesy of Tisha Mccuiston

Page 282 / Travel photos
courtesy of Quan Trinh

INDEX